ABOUT THE AUTHOR

Emma De Vita is features editor on *Management Today*. During her years on the magazine, she has spent time in jail, watching catwalk shows and travelling to San Paolo, New York and Mumbai all in the name of business journalism, for which she has won a number of awards. Her articles have also appeared in the *Sunday Times*, the *Guardian* and the *Financial Times*.

'Ideal as a companion on a flight, or to dip into for a bit of pre-meeting inspiration. Well done *MT*.'

Stefan Stern, *Financial Times*

'Practical, inspirational and insightful. An invaulable guide that every aspiring high flyer can learn from.'

Chey Garland CBE,
Veuve Cliquot Businesswoman of the Year

THE MANAGEMENT MASTERCLASS

Great business ideas without the hype

not just business as usual

THE MANAGEMENT
MASTERCLASS

Great business ideas without the hype

Edited by Emma De Vita

headline
business plus

First published in 2010 by
HEADLINE PUBLISHING GROUP

1

Cataloguing in Publication Data is available from the British Library

ISBN 978 0 7553 6014 7

Typeset in Bembo and Avenir by Susie Bell, www.f-12.co.uk

Printed and bound in Great Britain by
CPI Mackays

Headline's policy is to use papers that are natural, renewable and recyclable products and
made from wood grown in sustainable forests. The logging and manufacturing processes
are expected to conform to the environmental regulations of the country of origin.

HEADLINE PUBLISHING GROUP
An Hachette UK Company
338 Euston Road
London NW1 3BH

www.headline.co.uk
www.hachette.co.uk

CONTENTS

ACKNOWLEDGEMENTS

Thanks to all *Management Today* contributors, past and present. With particular thanks to Octavius Black and The Mind Gym for 'Your Route to the Top', Alexander Garrett for 'Crash Course' and 'Interview Time', Helen Kirwan-Taylor for 'Are You Suffering From', John Morrish for 'Words-Worth', Stefan Stern for 'Masterclass' and 'Ten Vital Tough Values', Alastair Dryburgh for 'Don't You Believe It', Miranda Kennett for her contribution to 'Are You Confident Enough?', Steve Lodge for his '25 Cashflow Tips', which featured in *Accelerator*, Robert Allison, Managing Director of Expense Reduction Analysts, for 'Ten Ways to Cut Your Costs by 20%', David Waller for his own contributions to 'Brainfood', Keith Parish for his help with the proofing and Patrick Regout for his illustrations.

With special thanks to John Moseley for his kind understanding, Robert Kirby for his superb trainers, and Matthew Gwyther for helping to make this happen. A thank you to Simon Lees and the rest of the *MT* team. Finally, SK for his love and humour.

FOREWORD

What makes good management? Much ink has been spilt, hundreds of conferences held and thousands of presentations given in answering that question. Well, there is no holy grail, no silver bullet that delivers perfect management. But, there are a few clear principles that managers can follow to avoid disaster – and hopefully build success.

Good management obviously starts with good leaders. Good leaders understand that to inspire people you do not – must not – try to control them. You need to set a clear direction, a simple strategy and high ambitions. Then you need to stick to your strategy, delegate and encourage risk taking. Successful businesses do not have one leader; they create a team in which there are scores of leaders.

To achieve this you need to build trust within your team. Trust is built on shared values. At Tesco we have two such values: be first for customers and treat people how we like to be treated; and the belief that every person in our team, no matter what he or she does, deserves respect for the contribution they make towards meeting our shared goals. The latter is critical to building trust. So too is your attitude to mistakes. Mistakes happen, they are the price you must pay for allowing people to take risks. It is better to learn a lesson from a mistake, than never to take a risk at all.

Delegation does not mean abdication of responsibility. Far from it. Our managers don't simply know how the business functions, they also have a passion for understanding how it's perceived by our customers. What needs to change to keep our customers loyal? How can a process be made simpler to keep costs low? How can you motivate people to make change routine?

Change is something that challenges every business, especially retailers. Good managers know that as the world changes – recession, a new trend, a competitor's sales drive – you too must change, meet new targets and up your game. So while strategy is important, implementation is critical.

At Tesco we have a balanced scorecard approach where we set measurements and targets against all our core strategic objectives – and give this to every store. That means our very large goals are met by millions of small actions in all our stores – and everyone can see how they are contributing. Everyone knows what success means for him or her personally, the individual store and the company as a whole. This drives change and motivates our team.

Finally, an inspirational manager's ambitions are bold, they break new ground, they are not defined by the competition, but by a desire to be the best. For these managers the world is full of possibilities and opportunities, not problems. Focus on the customer, unafraid to ask uncomfortable questions about the business, happy to celebrate the team's success – these are the qualities that mark managers out.

While I would never claim to have all these attributes, I have been fortunate to work for years in a strong team. So while there is no holy grail, you can learn from other people's experience – and mistakes. And that, in the end, is the most important rule that every manager must remember: however good you are, there is always room for improvement.

Never stop learning. This book provides a valuable, no-nonsense approach to management, giving clear, practical advice on what good management is.

Sir Terry Leahy, chief executive, Tesco plc

INTRODUCTION

Do you think of yourself as having a career or a job? Do you want to get ahead or is it about the nine to five? Are you ambitious or do you want to keep your head down and just take the pay cheque at the end of each month? If you're engaged in your work and want to get ahead, then this book will give you the leg-up that you need. If, on the other hand, you don't care for success, then perhaps this isn't for you.

Management Today may be the UK's leading monthly business magazine but it isn't just about 'business as usual'. We don't regurgitate cutting-edge business school thinking or shout about the latest front line development without first giving it intelligent consideration. We pride ourselves in giving you practical, no-nonsense advice, whether you're a chief executive, a graduate trainee or a fledgling entrepreneur. If you need advice on becoming the best, no matter where you are on the career ladder, then we've got it covered.

This book draws on some of the best advice that we've given our readers, as well as providing some brand new ideas. The emphasis is on the stuff you need to know to get on with your everyday job, whether it's learning how to become a better decision-maker or how to get that promotion. It's about climbing the greasy pole but having fun on the way up. It's for those of you just starting out but with the ambition to get ahead, and those of you who are old hands at managing but are after a spot of light refreshment.

If you read this book from cover to cover then we hope you'll learn something useful for every aspect of your job. If on the other hand it just sits on your desk to provide emergency advice during tricky situations, then we hope we can get you out of your scrape. The aim is to give you a masterclass in management that will become your career companion.

The book is divided into five chapters. The first chapter – 'You' – is about the personal values and skills you need to develop if you're to become a brilliant manager. Are you confident enough? Are you emotionally intelligent? It's also about what you need to know when you're actually in the hot seat. So, do you know how to delegate? Can you make a decision? And can you inspire those who work for you?

The second chapter – 'Us' – is about recognising that a manager cannot work in isolation. Your success will be measured as much by your team's performance as your own. If you can foster a 'we're in it together' attitude by creating high trust and a high-morale environment, you'll be able to get the best from your team. Who knows? You might even be able to give them a sense of fulfilment. A happy team will go the extra mile for you. There's also advice on how to deal with the meat of managerial work – interviewing recruits, conducting appraisals, running meetings, and managing staff who aren't in the office.

The third chapter, meanwhile, is all about 'The Numbers'. Although many of you might feel entirely at ease with budgets and cash-flow, there will be others who feel queasy at the mere mention of the word 'spreadsheet'. Don't worry. We give some hands-on managerial tips on how to get the budget you want, and how to beg for more resources when you don't. There's also a section on pay, which will provide an enlightening read.

The fourth chapter – 'The Challenges' – should help soothe some of your management headaches, because it's all about problem-solving, from dealing with difficult people to rescuing a project that has gone awry. Plus, there's a section to help you when the going gets really tough, including unexpected crises, redundancy and recession. Keep calm and carry on.

The final chapter – 'Getting Ahead' – completes the circle by focusing once again on you. Not you the manager but you the individual who wants to get ahead. What is it that you need to know to become successful in your chosen career? How do you stand out from the crowd? How can you excel in a job interview? And finally, what are the obstacles you should be looking out for, and what hot tips can you discover that will help you get to your destination?

Management Today does what it says on the tin. We've been writing about and leading the way on management since 1966, and have charted every trend and idea on the subject. We're proud of the fact that we were the first magazine to use the term 'work/life balance' in the 1990s, as well as an early advocate of corporate social responsibility. Perhaps we're less sure of the success of the 'femanager' neologism we coined back in the mid-1970s to describe the emergence of the female manager, just before Margaret Thatcher came to power.

If a young manager from the 1960s could be beamed down to sit alongside their twenty-first-century peer, they would find that their job had changed considerably. The typing pool, the smoking, the boys' club have all disappeared. What would those snappy dressers have thought of wearing jeans to work? But then fifty years is a long time. Try just taking the last decade of the twentieth century. It wasn't until 1997 that a FTSE 100 company had its first female CEO. Working from home was a new phenomenon; e-mail was kicking off but the emphasis was still on a command and control, hierarchical approach to management.

The noughties started to change all that. Technology democratised communication, so that a CEO who blogged or tweeted was on the same web footing as the new graduate trainee. A shift in the way we thought about work and our careers meant that most of us expected our jobs to fulfil us. All of a sudden, bosses became responsible for making their staff happy. Not only that, but their style of management had to become emotionally aware. Respect wasn't only demanded from the chief executive – it became the right of everyone working in every organisation.

All these changes, compounded by a recession that was a new experience for many young managers, mean that there's a lot to keep pace with. View this book as a shortcut to becoming a brilliant manager in the twenty-first century. It doesn't claim to be comprehensive; it's meant to be kept to hand so that when you find yourself in need of some help or inspiration, you can delve in and get the necessary information. And we'll entertain you while you're learning.

The 2010s will no doubt bring more new management buzzwords, theories, heroes and heroines. The global downturn and national recession that we found ourselves in will have its own impact on the way we think about our work, our careers, and what we want from our managers. It's impossible to predict what tomorrow's world will look like but the best preparation for any manager is to keep an open mind and listen to what the people around you are saying. That, and read *Management Today*, of course.

Emma De Vita
January 2010

YOU

HAVE YOU GOT WHAT IT TAKES?

No one is a natural born manager. You don't pop into the world, BlackBerry in one hand, umbilical cord in the other, ordering the midwife to get a move on. Becoming a brilliant manager can only be learnt on the job. But you can get a head start. And if you know how to be authentic, are confident, emotionally intelligent and a good communicator, then you're already halfway there.

Management is not about swaggering around the office making demands of your quailing minions while brown-nosing the chief executive. You can also forget trying to impress people by speaking in business jargon – that managerial approach went out the window a long time ago, along with smoking at your desk, having a secretary, in fact, having your own office at all.

ARE YOU AUTHENTIC?

'Find out who you are and do it on purpose'
DOLLY PARTON SAID IT

The first rule of being a brilliant manager is realising that you don't have to be a superhero to get it right. Don't be scared to just be yourself – your team will respect you more if they see that you are a lot like them. They'll lose respect for you if you pretend to be someone you're not.

But don't take 'authenticity' the wrong way. It isn't about going big on the whole San Fran love 'n' peace thing, man. It's about having enough self-awareness to know what your strengths are and how to use them to your best advantage; and what your weaknesses are, and how best to reveal them cleverly – or remedy them quickly.

WORDS-WORTH: AUTHENTICITY

To be authentic is to be real, genuine, trustworthy. An authentic person is true to his or her own character. The word arrived in English in the fourteenth century via French and Latin from Greek, where authentikos *meant something like 'having authority'. Those who preach authenticity in business insist that consumers will seek out the genuine. What's more, in the online age, they can easily talk to each other and pass on their experiences, meaning that bogus products are hard to hide. For an individual, to be authentic is to be yourself, but it's more practical to concentrate on keeping your promises. It is easy to be cynical about authenticity, which lends itself so well to an old joke: the secret of success is authenticity; if you can fake that, you've got it made.*

'I wouldn't say I was the best manager in the business, but I was in the top one'
BRIAN CLOUGH SAID IT

YOUR ROUTE TO THE TOP...
HOW TO BE AUTHENTIC

Sell your differences. Authenticity is not just about knowing yourself but also how you communicate that to others. Bill Gates plays on his 'geekiness' and is viewed as a passionate and knowledgeable techie.

Remember your roots. Niall FitzGerald, former chairman at Unilever, speaks often and with insight about his Irish heritage and the influence of his mother on both his moral and political views. Share the experiences in your early life or career that have had the greatest impact on you.

Break the mould. Rather than following the 'GE way', the 'Branson way' or the 'Harvard MBA way', find your own way.

Go beyond your comfort zone. Practise adapting to your new surroundings while remaining yourself. Whether you take on a challenging project or secondment abroad, find out who you really are.

Walk the talk. You will never gain credibility if you fail to live by your own convictions. Eliot Spitzer, ex-governor of New York, spent his tenure trying to remove prostitution and other lawless activities from the city streets. Then he was caught out as a client of an up-market brothel. You must practise what you preach.

ARE YOU CONFIDENT ENOUGH?

It takes courage to be authentic, and you won't be able to pull it off unless you have a healthy level of self-confidence. Not too much, and not too little...

You're under-confident if you...

1 Have been on the same salary for more than two years
2 Assume everyone else is more intelligent than you
3 Whisper rather than speak up
4 Avoid eye contact when talking
5 Have a handshake like a wet flounder
6 Try to take up as little space as possible
7 Believe your opinion doesn't matter
8 Would rather have teeth pulled than make a presentation
9 Fail to recognise your growing competence
10 Allow your fear to prevent you from doing what you most want

...and what to do about it

1 Act confident and only you will know you're not
2 Turn up the volume and reduce the speed at which you talk
3 Good eye contact and pausing when you've finished a sentence gives you gravitas
4 Banish fidgeting, hair-twiddling and other non-confident body language
5 Replace tentative words (maybe, perhaps, might) with positive, vigorous ones (will, definitely, absolutely)
6 Each time you tackle a scary situation, praise yourself for what you did well and chalk the rest up to experience
7 Write down a long list of what you're good at and read it when you're feeling wobbly
8 Recognise that even the most outwardly confident people sometimes get butterflies
9 Dress confident – it'll boost your morale

10 Before a difficult conversation, think of a past situation that worked out well. The good memory will make you feel more positive

You're over-confident if you...

1 Believe you are brighter than everyone else
2 Put your feet on the desk
3 Trust your own gut feelings at all times
4 Love the sound of your own voice
5 Assume everybody fancies you
6 Crush fingers when you're shaking hands
7 Never listen to other people's opinions
8 Never miss the chance to hog the limelight
9 Claim negative feedback is lying rivalry
10 Believe your own positive PR

...and what to do about it

1 Adjust the volume – downwards
2 Tone down the language
3 Sit back and listen. Don't interrupt
4 Pause before you speak to allow brain to engage before mouth
5 Ensure you have data to back up your assertions
6 See how people with quiet power operate
7 Reduce the risk of bad decisions by consulting those with experience
8 Get frequent feedback to better understand the effect you have on others
9 Admit you might be wrong – it's a sign of strength, not weakness
10 Smile. Help others to relax

ARE YOU SUFFERING FROM...
HUBRIS SYNDROME?

Hubris Syndrome is not necessarily something we're born with but, like a fatty diet, it quickly makes us bloated. The theory is that the closer we get to power, the more our brain starts to feed on it. Pretty soon we're like heroin addicts, needing more and more of it or we fall apart. Symptoms include the habit of seeing the world as an ersatz stage on which to exercise power; a messianic manner; excessive confidence in our own talent; and a belief that we are accountable only to God. Sufferers tend to be impulsive, restless, reckless and often isolated from friends. Hubris Syndrome is most dangerous where checks and balances are few. A sceptical spouse or even confident friends can curb tendencies, but the more severe the affliction, the less likely one is to seek other opinions. By making it a fully fledged medical disorder, psychiatrists hope to protect the world from power-crazy politicians. The problem is that hubris can double as charm. It's not until we're in power, ordering rose petals to be cast in front of us as we walk, that everyone else realises they screwed up.

ARE YOU EMOTIONALLY INTELLIGENT?

Forget about IQ, these days it's all about EQ – or Emotional Intelligence. It's essentially about how good you are at reading others' emotions, and how in control you are of your own. It's not necessarily about being 'soft' or 'nice', it's about using feelings to your best advantage.

Masterclass in Emotional Intelligence:
What is it?

Oh, don't bother me now, stupid. Can't you see I'm busy? Sorry, slight lapse there. Emotional Intelligence is a label to sum up the range of interpersonal skills and responses that form our public persona. It is often contrasted with existing notions of intelligence – not IQ, but EQ. Emotionally intelligent people show empathy and tact, are self-aware and in control of their feelings. They are the deft operators in our pressurised modern world, rising to the top while making as few enemies as possible.

Where did it come from?

In 1995, the US psychologist Daniel Goleman published his ground-breaking work, *Emotional Intelligence*, a book that, fifteen years later, is still winning converts. In a chapter entitled 'Managing with Heart', Goleman argued for a more considered, empathetic style of management. 'Too many managers have poorly mastered the crucial art of feedback,' he wrote. 'Leadership is not domination, but the art of persuading people to work towards a common goal.' The book coincided with the emergence of the 'new economy', where approachability and openness were in and hierarchy was out (as were, sadly, profits).

ARE YOU A GREAT COMMUNICATOR?

Your purpose in life as a manager is to get other people to do things for you, and you can't do this without communicating with them. Brilliant managers are excellent at getting their

Ten Ways to Listen

1 Make time and take time
2 Clear your mind
3 Give your undivided attention
4 Don't interrupt
5 Ask what they mean
6 Check body language
7 Keep your opinions to yourself
8 Check what they really feel
9 Hear what's not being said
10 Play back what you've heard

message across, be it through clear orders or subtle persuasion and appreciate that communication is a two-way process. Most people underestimate the importance of listening but the best managers are the ones with the biggest ears.

The art of knowing how to hold a conversation with someone is coming under threat. We may be expert texters and tweeters but are we losing the ability to make face-to-face conversation?

DO IT RIGHT: MAKE CONNECTIONS

Find your shared interests. You don't have to limit conversation to work-chat; talking about the latest footie scores or *The X Factor* results doesn't make you seem unprofessional – just friendly.

Make them feel special. When you do make the effort to strike up a conversation, give your colleague all your attention. Listen carefully and don't get distracted.

Uncover their appeal. By getting to know your colleagues, you'll soon find out what it is about them that attracts others.

Keep your opinions to yourself. Don't turn a friendly chat into an emotionally turbulent and heavy discussion. It's not your job to hog the limelight; learn to keep quiet and listen to them.

Make your own contribution. Move the conversation along by adding your own examples or anecdotes to their stories.

Brilliant managers also tend to be first-class persuaders. They have the ability to make people want to do the task they've set them by letting them think it was their idea in the first place, and that they're the only person in the world up to the job.

YOUR ROUTE TO THE TOP...
PEACEFUL PERSUASION

Have a plan. Consider the route that you are going to take and how to deal with resistance. But be ready to change it.

Know your audience. Discover their real concerns and interests, whether that might be wanting a promotion or to close a deal quickly.

Put them in a good mood. Gentle flattery is surprisingly effective. They will be more open to persuasion if they feel favourable towards you.

Choose your moment. Be conscious of their frame of mind. Seize the good moments as they appear.

Do as they do. Match their body language (if they lean forward, do the same). This will put them at ease and encourage a stronger emotional connection.

What's in it for them? Show that it's in their best interest to agree with you. Convince them that they are on to a good thing, where you'll both share in the success.

Describe the end result. Be sure to demonstrate how the new situation will be better than the present one.

Get them to do the work. Ask questions that guide them to your conclusion. People are more likely to agree if they feel that they've come to the conclusion – at least partly – themselves.

Make your case. State all the facts; be clear about the pros and cons. Offer solutions that will resolve their concerns and turn weaknesses into strengths.

Do them a favour. Tell them what you will do for them in return. They might well feel indebted to you and therefore more likely to agree.

Use your allies. Refer to the views of someone whose opinion they care about. People are more likely to think or do something if others they respect do too.

Having managerial mojo – being authentic, confident, emotionally intelligent, and a great communicator – is only half the story when it comes to being a brilliant boss. The other half is about being chucked in at the deep end and learning how to swim.

KNOWING WHAT TO DO

Brilliant managers know how to behave while in the hot seat, whether that's in an air traffic control tower, a recording studio or a hospital ward. They can get stuff done, delegate well, motivate and inspire the people that work for them. They also make good decisions (and learn from the bad ones), and are in 'the loop'. Most importantly, they don't take themselves too seriously.

But first things first. You need to look the part. Image is everything, so if you're having a bad nasal hair day, it's time to get some sartorial help.

Ten Ways to Dress for Success

1 Take out your tongue stud
2 Think *West Wing*, not *Sex in the City*
3 Look conservative. With a small 'c'
4 Knock 'em dead, but not with your perfume
5 Avoid novelty fashion
6 Accessorise carefully (you're not Pat Butcher)
7 Stick with the office dress code
8 Aim for slightly smarter than needed
9 Don't out-dress your boss
10 It's all in the details

CAN YOU GET STUFF DONE?

One of the tell-tale signs of a brilliant manager is the buzz that surrounds them – people get excited just by being near them. Their magical sense of urgency is infectious, yet their energy is disciplined and focused – they know how to get stuff done. Procrastinators they are not.

ARE YOU SUFFERING FROM... SOMEDAY SYNDROME?

Procrastinators know when they are putting things off (e.g. the boss has come in for the third time looking for the report that was due yesterday, and is not happy). Someday Syndrome is the thought that one day I will: start my own business, write a book or visit Rome. It stokes up the desire without necessarily demanding any work on your part. Dreaming is, after all, accepting that things will never happen. With Someday Syndrome, sufferers really believe they will

CRASH COURSE IN...
HAVING RAZOR SHARP FOCUS

Work out what you want to achieve. Sort that out and it suddenly lends meaning to everything you do.

Slow down. Instead of racing to cross each job off the list so that you can get on to the next, give the task in hand the time it deserves.

Keep a tidy desk. The fewer distractions around you, the easier it is to focus. The same goes for your computer too.

Build a routine. Work out how and when you work best: are you better at doing mundane stuff early, or is it best to leave that till the afternoon, when your mind starts winding down?

Approach tasks properly. When making a presentation, most people engage a different part of their personality than the one they use down the pub. Yet when approaching tasks in the office, we tend to go at it in whatever mood we happen to be. Find the right side of your character to suit the task.

Get it out of your head. This may mean a to-do list, a comprehensive list of calls, or logging actions on to your PDA, and not moving on until the first is complete.

Don't camp in your inbox. Switch the e-mail ping-alert off, and check your messages only a few times a day. And don't go near your personal mail until you've done some work first.

Have fun. If you genuinely enjoy what you're doing, it becomes easier to stick at it. Reward yourself when you finish things.

do it, but not right now. They might go as far as to write lists and join clubs; they just never get beyond that. Many coaches specialise in this disorder, often by getting clients to start tackling Someday today. Someone wishing to get fit must put their trainers on that minute and go. The get–going school of thought often works, but it tends to shift the Someday Syndrome elsewhere.

Ten Ways to Get Something Done

1 Accept that it needs doing
2 Don't think about it, do it
3 Remember: it's your job
4 Do it now
5 Do it well – within reason
6 Find a way to enjoy it
7 Smile while you do it
8 Reward yourself afterwards
9 Think of the money
10 Delegate

ARE YOU SUFFERING FROM... EXECUTIVE DYSFUNCTION?

Do you start a project, then immediately immerse yourself in another? Is your idea of forward planning deciding where to go for lunch? If so, you may have the latest disability *du jour*: Executive Dysfunction. The dishevelled manager who permanently apologises for forgetting meetings is not lazy: he has abnormalities in his CEO – the control centre of the brain that enables you to maintain a mental image of a destination.

Those with a poor CEO may function brilliantly if their PA does everything for them, but ask them to plan a holiday, and you'll be lucky if they remember which holiday. Information simply vanishes from their mind. Treatment involves taking the same stimulant drugs as hyperactive children or strengthening organisational skills. Alternatively, sufferers can substitute their auxiliary frontal lobe with that of another human being.

YOUR ROUTE TO THE TOP...
HANDLING INTERRUPTIONS

Find out if it's necessary. Ask what they want, whether it has to be you, and if it has to be now. How we treat an interruption affects not only how our time is spent now, but also the likelihood that we will be interrupted later.

Relish the right interruptions. They can be a source of great insight, creativity and strong relationships. Or they can simply wake us up. The trick is to spot quickly whether it's a good or bad interruption and act accordingly.

Recognise what's in it for you. Does it make you feel helpful or supportive when people come to ask for your advice or approval?

Help people to help themselves. When someone asks you for guidance, coach them to solve the problem alone rather than taking on the task yourself. It may take longer now, but it will save you time later.

Change your default setting. If you always say yes immediately, leave a pause before you agree. Use those moments to ask yourself whether it's in your own best interests to do so.

Do unto others... Be sensitive about how and when you interrupt other people. If you aren't being a great role model, don't be surprised if others follow your poor example.

Explain your position. For those who persist in interrupting, make sure they are aware of the effect their behaviour has on your time. Then fix a specific point in the day or week to discuss all their issues.

Be firm. Get used to saying 'no' or at least 'not now' every once in a while. The interrupters may then seek out someone who is a softer touch.

CAN YOU DELEGATE?

The brilliant manager knows how to delegate well (and without feeling guilty). It's one of the hardest parts of the job and there's no room at the top for control freaks or micromanagers.

WORDS-WORTH: MICROMANAGEMENT

Microelectronics is a great success. Nanotechnology is even sexier – and smaller. But don't bother with micromanagement. No one likes it. If you think that God is in the details and you can't help noticing the little things, like the poor quality of new paperclips, you're a natural micromanager. Since appearing in America, c.1979, micromanagement – defined as interference and excessive control – has always been a bad thing. In truth, while micromanaging has its charms for some, there's no one in the world who wants a micromanager as their boss.

ARE YOU SUFFERING FROM...
ANAL RETENTION?

We all know Freud was obsessed with toilet training. One theory was that children who did not master the art of elimination got, well, constipated. This turned a normal child into an obsessive and tidy adult preoccupied with petty details. Every office has an Anal Retentive. They're the one with the matching sharpened pencils lined up on their desk and the iron in their briefcase. They spellcheck e-mails in their inbox, pick the lint off their aeroplane seat and go through everyone's expenses with a calculator. At home, Anal Retentives organise soup cans alphabetically and label drawers. They may be constipated socially as well – i.e., they're not exactly a barrel of laughs. Certain drugs can loosen them up, as can cognitive behavioural therapy, but no one wants an anal expulsive accountant.

History lessons: Delegate to succeed

The Krays started out in the 1950s, running protection rackets from a dingy snooker hall in east London. Through a mixture of robbery and violence, they acquired a small empire of London clubs and properties and, in a clever bit of brand positioning, became a visible part of the 'Swinging Sixties' scene. But they kept their hands dirty with the day-to-day running of their criminal empire - personally murdering their enemies, George Cornell and Jack 'the Hat' McVitie. Less blood-thirsty managers often fall at the same hurdle: despite having a large number of staff at their disposal, they find it hard to let go of the day-to-day stuff and concentrate on the bigger picture. For the Krays, poor delegation caused their downfall. Sentenced to life imprisonment, their 'firm' quickly collapsed. If you want to build a lasting empire, employ people you can trust and let them do their jobs.

YOUR ROUTE TO THE TOP...
DYNAMIC DELEGATION

Make sure you know why you're delegating. If it's because someone else can do it better or it will save your time, great. But effective delegation takes time, so if you're just being lazy or the task is small, do it yourself.

Choose whom you delegate to carefully. Select someone who has core skills and the motivation to complete the challenge well. Choosing those who will put up least resistance is tempting but misguided.

Discuss what needs to be done. Ask questions: What are the problems likely to be? How will you start? Who else will you involve? Check they understand what you want by asking them to paraphrase it back to you.

Set boundaries. Make it clear what they can do themselves (draft the report) and what should be checked (send it to the CEO).

Set up support mechanisms. E.g., places and people to go to if they get stuck.

Give them space to think and act for themselves. They are not you, and so will not do it in the same way.

Give constructive feedback at regular reviews. Tell them what they are doing well and be specific about what could improve.

Review after the event. This will clarify how you could have delegated more effectively and assist them in seeing where they can improve, thus making future delegation easier for both parties.

CAN YOU INSPIRE?

You may not feel particularly inspirational at 9 o'clock on a Monday morning, but your team are sure to be looking to you for motivation, encouragement and direction. Think of yourself as the office Mr Motivator, leotard, bumbag, and all.

Ten Ways to Motivate

1 Be motivated yourself
2 Understand what motivates your team
3 Give them a challenge
4 Treat them with respect
5 Listen to them
6 Help them learn
7 Stick up for them
8 Let them do things their way
9 Reward achievement
10 Say thank you

Ten Ways to Inspire

1 Be clear in your own goals
2 Tell a compelling story
3 Give people a real challenge
4 Treat people with respect
5 Listen to your people's ideas
6 Understand your people's concerns
7 Protect your people from interference
8 Keep calm in a crisis
9 Always have a plan
10 Fight for what you believe in

CAN YOU MAKE A (GOOD) DECISION?

A manager's job is to make decisions. A weak and feeble decision-maker will soon lose the respect of their team. Although it can be tough to make a decision under pressure and without all the information at your fingertips, it is better to act and then switch tactic as the situation changes, than to remain paralysed with indecision.

Good judgement can't be easily taught but is an essential quality of an excellent decision-maker.

Ten Ways to Better Judgement

1 Know what you want
2 Get good information
3 Separate fact from assumption
4 Don't be unsettled by uncertainty
5 Be led by the outcome, not your tastes
6 Keep an open mind
7 Find the lessons in your mistakes
8 Learn from others
9 Empathise
10 Remember: you're in control

YOUR ROUTE TO THE TOP...
TAKE THAT DECISION

Get started. Ask yourself whether you can resolve a problem there and then. If so, do it. If not, follow Einstein's approach: 'Make it as simple as possible, but no simpler.'

Define the problem. In one sentence, write down what you have to make a decision about.

Explore what's involved. Who and what will be affected, when and where will the outcome be implemented, and why do you even need to make the decision?

Consider different perspectives. How would your boss approach it? What would your competitor do? Approaching the problem from different angles helps you to understand the facts objectively.

Picture your ideal outcome. Whether it's securing a six-figure contract or starting up your own business, how can your choice bridge the gap between the present and your perfect outcome?

Challenge your assumptions. The merit of your decision is based on the process you've followed, not just the outcome. Make sure it's foolproof.

Make your choice. Bring all the facts together and write a list of the pros and cons. Then make your decision and stick to it. Nothing can ever be 100 per cent, so go with the best-looking option.

Make it happen. Take a flexible approach and strike a balance between planning and adjusting: signing a new contract is not signing your life away. Respect your decision, but don't be a slave to it.

Don't restrict yourself. Why have just one? Over the course of your career you should benefit from a range of experts. Have a group of advisers and dip in and out, depending on your need.

It's one thing to take a decision but another to make a good decision…

CRASH COURSE IN...
MAKING GOOD DECISIONS

Frame it. The first step is to define the decision. Most decisions go wrong because the wrong issue requiring a decision is identified – the symptoms rather than the true causes are addressed. Decisions can be stimulated by three situations: opportunity, problem resolution and crisis. They need to be framed in terms of a well-defined problem, which usually means travelling from the current clearly described situation to the desired situation.

Whose decision? Ask yourself: is it important to make a decision? And if I don't make the decision, will it be made by someone else? If your answer is yes to the first and no to the second, you either have to take the decision or delegate it.

Understand your mind. Most decision-making depends on two main processes. In pattern-recognition, people base the decision on what they think is a similar situation, often from previous experience. And emotional tagging involves an emotional investment being attached to particular outcomes.

Question your objectivity. In each case, you may have in-built biases you aren't aware of. You favour a particular course of action because that's how it was done in your previous job, or perhaps you have a personal interest in the decision: e.g., relocating an office nearer your own home. If there is a risk of bias creeping in, you need to introduce safeguards that will counterbalance it.

Sharpen your skills. Consider the widest range of options. People find it easier to look at one plan at a time, but you can progress and evaluate several simultaneously. Research has demonstrated the value of counter-factual thinking. Thinking about the opposite helps us make better decisions.

THE MANAGEMENT MASTERCLASS

Share the burden. Form a decision-making group, and subject its activity to oversight – say, by the board. Firms good at decision-making share the process and allow dissent along the way.

Don't write off intuition. We make certain types of decision better intuitively than analytically. Nimble firms leave day-to-day decision-making with instinctive leaders who can make rapid calls on most issues, but subject difficult and bias-ridden decisions to a procedural method.

Do say: 'We have a comprehensive approach to cover all our strategic decision-making requirements.'

Don't say: 'Ip, dip, penny, chip…'

ARE YOU SUFFERING FROM… COROLLARY SYNDROME?

Corollary Syndrome is what happens to people who have just made a big decision. They have just bought a new Bentley, so conclude it is the only car of choice. Also called synchronicity, CS is about self-centredness. The executive, having thought of taking up golf, hears people talking about it at a dinner and concludes that because everyone important is playing golf, he must make it a mandatory skill for prospective employees. CS can be innocent but it can also turn into policy. What starts out as a personal choice ('I won't use internal e-mail') can soon turn into the company's mission statement. Treatment is to demand evidence for the supposition (that everyone is playing golf) and to be aware of sentences starting with 'I've noticed that everyone is…' Sufferers often don't realise the extent of their narcissism but can be treated with shock tactics, such as: 'You're wrong!'

When you do make the wrong decision, be brave, admit your mistake and carry on. Your team will respect you more for it.

Ten Ways to Admit You're Wrong

1 Understand it's for the best
2 Don't stress about it
3 See it as a stepping-stone to success
4 Do it promptly
5 Be honest
6 Keep a level tone of voice
7 Hold eye contact
8 Don't grovel
9 Put it behind you
10 Don't repeat the mistake

ARE YOU IN THE LOOP?

A brilliant manager will always have the ear of the people who matter. Their ability to build a broad network of contacts inside and outside the organisation means that not only are they able to influence those above them, but also be party to business rumours that can serve them well. Networking isn't just for ladies who lunch...

WORDS-WORTH: NETWORK

Real networks (of computers, phones or people) can and will go wrong, but the word itself won't let you down. It stands for everything today's management aspires to: it's as light as a feather but as strong as a hawser; it holds things together but lets them move; it expands, it shrinks, painlessly. Comforting in hard times, cool when the heat is on, the network is the string vest of modern business.

It is a metaphor, of course. A real network is something made like a net — a mesh of rope or string for catching things. 'Net' goes back into the depths of the Indo-European languages but 'network' occurred first in English in Tyndale's Bible of 1526, where it describes a brass lattice. Later, it referred to natural structures that looked like nets, then to things linked in the same way: blood vessels, processes, relationships, radio stations. The verb 'to network' is a product of US feminism, which taught businesswomen to network to sidestep existing male networks. Don't worry if your network is full of holes. It's meant to be.

CRASH COURSE IN...
NETWORKING

Online should complement offline networking. If you meet someone interesting at an event, keep in touch via LinkedIn.

Keep your personal and work lives separate. Don't add colleagues as Facebook friends unless they really are friends. If your boss or someone else from work wants to be your friend, reject them and don't apologise. Alternatively, just ignore them. Consider using a professional networking site for work networking; keep Facebook for social stuff.

Join professional forums. Online is an easy way to raise your profile but watch discussion for a while before wading in with your own comments. Post using your real name.

Be careful with your comments. Don't slag off anyone or anything online. It could all come back to you as a nasty mess – remember, posted comments don't disappear overnight.

It pays to press the flesh. Networking doesn't just mean online. You've got to get yourself out and about in the real world. After you've accepted an invitation, do some research, so you know who'll be attending and who you can target. Read up on current affairs so that you can chip in with intelligent comment.

Put yourself about. You won't learn by sticking to people you know, so be confident about joining groups – you can help them as much as they can help you.

Listen. Others have needs too – help them to achieve their goals and they'll open up. They may even pass on an invaluable nugget of information. If someone's talking to you, don't let your eyes dart around looking for someone better.

Disengage graciously. Getting stuck with the wrong person can be a nuisance, but don't be rude about slipping away. Bring someone else into your conversation before making a break.

Remember names. Swap business cards, and discreetly jot names down if you have to. If you do forget, admit it quickly. If your must-meet contact is in demand, get someone to introduce you. Offer your card, ask the best way to contact them, then withdraw.

Follow-up. Always send an e-mail to a new contact – it doesn't have to be long. Just say how nice it was to meet. If you've promised them something, make sure you deliver.

US

WE'RE IN IT TOGETHER

'Coming together is a beginning; keeping together
is progress; working together is success'
HENRY FORD SAID IT

Enough about you; the only thing that should matter for a
manager is the 'us' factor. Not in the 'them and us' sense but
in the 'we're all in it together' sense. And when better to
capitalise on team spirit than during challenging times? The
recession – and the budget cuts, job losses and belt-tightening
that came with it – shifted the tectonic plates of our working
landscape. Some companies collapsed at the first hurdle;
others pulled together.

Many managers fell off their chairs on hearing that some
people willingly accepted reduced hours or pay freezes in the
hope that their organisation would emerge lean but fit to
make the most of the upswing. Was it a myth? No, but let's
face it, it wasn't the majority experience.

What made the difference between the companies that
made it and those that didn't was their success in fostering a
sense of loyalty, dedication and enjoyment among their staff
(yes! At work!). They wanted to put in the extra effort when
things went pear-shaped *and* wanted to stick around for when
the going got better again.

Employees are more likely to do a good – even excellent
– job if they are motivated by their own satisfaction; not

coerced into action by a dictatorial boss. This self-motivation (or 'employee engagement' as Human Resources would have us call it) brings good things, not least energy, productivity and innovation.

The engaged employee...

- Feels trusted, valued and empowered
- Gives their best; goes the extra mile
- Is loyal, motivated and enthusiastic
- Is an advocate for the company
- Understands the organisation's mission and their place in it; shares common values
- Is emotionally committed and personally involved

The engaged organisation...

- Performs better
- Has high staff retention
- Has sustained, long-term success
- Has a strong sense of purpose and identity
- Is highly energised, productive and innovative
- Has an attractive reputation

As a manager, it's your job to create this emotional attachment, but it's not so easy to build the environment that inspires this kind of engaged behaviour. Like getting a pair of giant pandas to breed in captivity, it's about putting the right conditions in place to ensure that the love-in actually happens.

You have to take the trouble to get to know the people with whom you spend eight or more hours of your day. Find

out what turns them on: is it money? An intellectual challenge? Closing a deal? Where do they want to go with their career? If you know what they enjoy doing, what their ambitions are, and can present a path that melds this with your own department's needs, then love will certainly be in the air — it might even be a match made in heaven.

CRASH COURSE IN...
KEEPING YOUR STAFF ENGAGED

Show that you have a plan. People are looking to you for leadership, to be more confident, more certain than they are.

Do it in person. Face-to-face communication is always best.

Involve your people. In good times, self-managing teams play a key role in creating engagement; in bad times, people still need to feel that they can make a difference and that the work they are doing is meaningful. Having some input is a huge factor in people's ownership and sense of engagement.

Redefine success. There's some evidence that success breeds engagement, but success measured by the usual parameters is hard to achieve in a climate where everything's going down the tubes. Don't make people responsible for things they can't control, but create a formula that should lead to success. And create targets they can hit.

Offer recognition. Whether it's through an employee-of-the-month scheme or just a pat on the back, show people that you appreciate the discretionary effort they put in.

Keep on celebrating. Applaud every small success, whether it's a piece of business gained, or a member of your team winning an award or passing an exam. And why not have a party, an awayday, or a dress-up-in-school-uniform day? People perform better with a smile on their face.

TRUST

Making sure that the people you manage feel fulfilled (even to the tiniest degree) is a tall order. It's all about empowerment – and, most importantly, trust. Creating an open, informal, no-blame culture is what you should aim for, but be prepared to crack the whip and dispense discipline when it's called for.

'I'm not upset that you lied to me, I'm upset that from now on I can't believe you'
FRIEDRICH NIETZSCHE SAID IT

'Right, now that a relationship of trust has been established, let's get down to business, shall we?'

Ten Ways to be a Trusted Manager

1 Be seen, be heard – and listen
2 Muck in from time to time
3 Be honest
4 Deliver bad news in person
5 Be consistent in your decisions
6 Don't have favourites
7 Praise when praise is due
8 Keep your promises
9 Admit your mistakes…
10 … but don't make too many of them

History lessons: Don't snoop

Before the Berlin Wall fell in 1989, East Germany's Ministry for State Security is said to have had a representative for every seven citizens (the Gestapo had one per 2,000, the KGB one per 5,830). The Stasi knew everything, from your reading habits to who you drank with. It tapped phone lines, traced citizens using radioactive material, and even collected smell samples from people's underpants. As the state's paranoia was cranked up, even innocuous acts became grounds for suspicion. The logic was: 'We're monitoring you, so you must be guilty of something.' But the drive for total control had the organisation creaking under its own weight: laid end-to-end, its exhaustive files would have stretched 180km. In this culture of suspicion, colleagues, friends and family were turning each other in. With tools such as e-mail, you don't need armies of informers and acres of files to know what your staff are up to. But it's best to let them get on with it. Build a culture of trust, not a wall between you and your team.

MORALE

Tight financial belts have squeezed out most traditional motivational carrots, but don't be tempted to give up on this essential duty. Try these morale-boosting alternatives for keeping your staff motivated:

Morale boosters...

1 Give up guessing. Ask staff what lights their fire, and observe for yourself their highs and lows.
2 Go public with praise. But keep it specific.
3 Beat boredom blues before they arrive. Maintain stimulation by using change and challenge.
4 Bring fun into the workplace. But keep staff involved. What makes you smile might make them throw a sickie.
5 Keep your own passion alive. Inspire by example rather than searching for the magic trick.

DO IT RIGHT:
MANAGE TEAM MORALE

Don't be a downer. Remember to promote your achievements. Tap into the spirit of what makes your company tick, and turn concerns into grounds for excitement.

Be open. If you don't tell your team what's going on, frankly and promptly, you'll lose trust, and they'll cook up their own less flattering version of events. A few home truths may even provide a timely kick up the rear, too.

Tell people how it will affect them. The bigger picture – like figures, redundancies and restructuring – is important, but don't neglect the little things: if you're removing canteen privileges and subsidised travel, say why.

Be consistent. Your bosses can't post phenomenal expenses claims when they're telling everyone else to tighten up.

Use the right channels. An honest e-mail from on high works for the big picture, but regular face-to-face chats are essential for getting the message to stick, for gauging staff reactions, and for offering reassurance.

Get people involved. Use the intranet to express your team's concerns, and ask for suggestions on how to increase efficiency. Offer modest rewards and just watch those hands rush to the pumps.

Use your imagination. Sober times don't mean that the celebrations should stop. The old champagne soirées may be out of the equation, but there are plenty of other options – from afternoon tea to camping trips.

SENSE OF PURPOSE

'The secret of success is consistency of purpose'
BENJAMIN DISRAELI SAID IT

You must provide your team with a real sense of purpose and an understanding of how they fit into your organisation's bigger picture. A manager is also a leader, and your team will look to you for direction – don't let them down. Tell them what their mission is, spell out the rules, but give them the freedom to get the job done in the best way they see fit.

Ten Ways to Create a Sense of Purpose

1 Create a mission
2 Make it convincing
3 Make sure everyone understands their part
4 Translate the mission into realistic goals
5 Reward success
6 Encourage friendly competitiveness
7 Keep focused
8 Remain ambitious
9 Never compromise on key principles
10 Be flexible in how you get there

Masterclass in Mission Statements:
What are they?

A good mission statement describes in a few words what your business or organisation is about, and what it intends to be. It will make sense, be written in plain language and will ring true with employees and customers. But those that are couched in abstract terms, or make ludicrous and unbelievable claims about your firm's destiny – Mission Impossible – do more harm than good. If your firm has a real 'reason to be', as Collins and Porras put it in their book *Built to Last*, you may not need a mission statement at all: 'A visitor could drop into your organisation from another planet and infer the vision without having to read it on paper.'

Where did they come from?

Mission statements are almost as old as modern business itself. Henry Ford was unequivocal: 'I will build a motor car for the great multitude ... when I'm through everybody will be able to afford one, and everyone will have one.' Mission accomplished. All through the last century businesses tried to express their goals in a phrase: 'To make people happy' (Disney); 'Made in Japan will mean something fine, not something shoddy' (Sony); 'Destroy Yamaha!' (Honda). Time's up for dodgy mission statements. Do you really want to have 'Passion' in the workplace? Do you need to boast about your 'Integrity'? And do you have to give these abstract nouns capital letters? Try the inverse mission statement test: if the opposite of what you say you are striving for is self-evidently undesirable – e.g., 'We aim to delight our customers' – there's no need to make a song and dance about it. Make it your mission to cut the crap.

YOUR ROUTE TO THE TOP...
CREATE CAN-DO SPIRIT

Get together. Research shows that a strong sense of purpose improves employee engagement and performance, as well as organisational success. Create a shared purpose in the form of a mission statement and your team will work better together.

Find the noble cause. Some of the most engaging missions are those linked to helping others. Corporate social responsibility is here to stay.

Make an emotional appeal. A focus like Google's 'Don't be evil' didn't appeal to everyone, but it drew like-minded people in. How do you want people to think, feel and behave?

Aim high. Set a clear and compelling target that will unify your efforts – and make it stretching. You may not win that national award, but in striving to be best you perform better.

Piggy-back. Select a well-known success and emulate it. Whether it's to be to the retail sector what Apple is to design, or to be the Warren Buffett of mortgage brokers, communicate what success looks like in a way that works for your team.

Create a healthy rivalry. A recruitment company organised its consultants into two teams. The mission was for each side to place more candidates than the other. The teams even had their own songs: 'Simply the Best' and 'Eye of the Tiger'; whenever they made a new placement, the relevant tune would boom across the office.

Open it up to the floor. Present your mission in draft form and invite everyone to critique and refine it. Then discuss how you can all make it happen. The shared sense of ownership will guide people's day-to-day work and decisions.

Make it real. Relate the mission to each individual's cares, concerns and role. What does the mission mean to them? As their situation changes, so will their connection to it.

You must give your staff autonomy and the freedom to do their work in the way they want. But this will only work if you set clear boundaries to what they can and cannot do. Don't be afraid to discipline them when they overstep the mark. It doesn't pay to be nice all of the time.

DO IT RIGHT:
CRACK THE WHIP

Build the right environment. A vibrant workplace – where everyone knows what they're doing, why, and how to do it – should set clear standards and keep discipline issues to a minimum.

Be a role model. Your authority will be lost if you're castigating someone for poor timekeeping but rolling in to meetings twenty minutes late yourself.

Get to the truth. Get everyone's version of events before taking further action. Persistent lateness may be due to family circumstances; could reports of harassment be a malicious rumour? Have a quiet word first.

Don't knock 'em down. A talking-to should get people back on track, not resentfully nursing a thick ear as though they've been naughty. Show them clearly the effect of their behaviour.

Do it promptly. Quash problems before they develop. Explain what improvements need to be made and over what period. Apply the same standards across the board. You can't let one bully off but punish another.

Go through the right channels. Treat the official course as a last resort. Give people advance warning of any hearing, a written explanation of disciplinary action taken, and make sure they understand the outcome.

Let them go. Persistent troublemaking may show someone doesn't belong in the job. Would both sides benefit if they took their expertise elsewhere? Find out how they got into that position, and don't let it happen again.

BE HAPPY

'Ask yourself if you are happy and you cease
to be so'
JOHN STUART MILL SAID IT

If you're working on building up trust in your team, have
boosted morale and have created a strong sense of purpose,
then focus your attention on finding out what makes your
staff feel satisfied in their jobs. Striving to make them feel
happy – or fulfilled – isn't a namby-pamby management aim
so don't be put off doing it by the sneering comments of less
emotionally intelligent peers. Happy staff work harder and
will go all out for you, so it'll be you who has the last laugh.

Ten Ways to Make Your People Happy

1 Treat them with respect
2 Listen to what they want
3 Avoid a 'blame' culture; allow failure
4 Be open and honest
5 Encourage initiative
6 Don't control
7 Give goals that stretch
8 Reward success but don't overpromise
9 Encourage friendships
10 Stamp out negativity

ARE YOU SUFFERING FROM...
THE HAWTHORNE EFFECT?

In a bid to improve productivity, a Chicago firm called Hawthorne Works once asked for volunteers to try different shift hours. After a few weeks the volunteers reported much higher levels of job satisfaction and corporate loyalty. The researchers asked them what it was exactly that worked: they had no idea. What seems to have made them so happy was the attention from colleagues and bosses for being picked for the experiment. Since the findings, countless bosses have discovered that giving employees praise and attention works better than, say, ignoring or maltreating them. Of course, this is all easy-peasy when things are running well and the company is posting profits. It all goes to hell in a handcart during difficult times. Someone suffering from (rather than basking in) the Hawthorne Effect calls attention to themselves when really they should keep their heads down. Typically, they crack inappropriate jokes in meetings and wear bright ties. This does get attention, but the wrong kind. It's much easier to sack someone who irritates you than someone you like who bites his or her lip. Still, the Hawthorne Effect is a valuable tool for bosses: if you can't offer someone a bonus, consider giving a nice bit of personal attention instead.

PRACTICALITIES

Philosophising about what good management is is one thing; dealing with the daily nitty-gritty is another. The way you handle interviews, appraisals and meetings is how you will be judged by your staff, and it's what your reputation is built on. So, it's important to act the part. For some, these tasks are the stuff of nightmares but they don't have to be the gremlins of your working life. With a bit of thought and preparation, you will be able to whizz the little monsters away at the flick of a switch.

FROM HELLO TO GOODBYE

It's important to get the entire employee cycle right, from the outset. Starting with how to promote someone, running a job interview, moving to induction, then appraisals, and finally exit interviews.

A key management vacancy is coming up and an internal appointment seems obvious. In your opinion, there's only one candidate, but colleagues are championing their own protégés. And you know there'll be resentment from those who miss out. So what's the best way to handle a promotion?

CRASH COURSE IN...
THE RIGHT WAY TO PROMOTE

Plan ahead. Succession plans have their limitations, because they close off options and are overtaken by events. The answer is to develop all your people on a continuous basis. Find out where individuals want to go in their career and provide them with the training, so that when a vacancy occurs, you have a choice of qualified people.

Think ahead. Don't assume that because a position is being vacated it must be filled in exactly the same form.

Profile and match. Too often, promotions are made on the basis of gut instinct, or even likeability, when a more scientific approach will yield better results. Draw up a profile of the job in question, looking at the skills, competencies and personality traits that it requires, then do the same with each of your candidates and find the best match.

Ask a colleague. If you involve other people in the selection process who will be internal customers of the person chosen, you will get a broad range of perceptions, and that person will have the support of those they will work with.

Let down the losers. If you know there are individuals who will be disappointed not to get the promotion, talk to them personally. You can use this as an opportunity to discuss their own aspirations and development needs, and what can be done to meet them. But if you feel they won't go any higher, it's only fair to tell them, so they won't labour on with false expectations.

Offer a lifeline. Throwing your promotions in at the deep end to see if they sink or swim might sound macho but it is a pitiful waste of resources. Making a transition from one level to another is challenging for most people, and support is vital. Immediate managers can provide coaching, while somebody more detached can act as mentor, providing a sounding board.

Do say: 'After extensive evaluation, Rachel has been chosen to fill this post on the strength of her relevant experience, her team-building skills and the respect in which she is held by colleagues.'

Don't say: 'I've been grooming Warren for this job since he started. If someone else thinks they could do it better, it's hard luck.'

So, you've got your shortlist of suitable candidates ready and lined up for interview. How do you make the most of this short amount of time to find out who's best for the job?

MIND YOUR MANNERS: HOLDING A JOB INTERVIEW

Know what you want. Define the post and the kind of person you need. This will save wasting everyone's time and help you plan decent questions.

Don't wing it. Sharp candidates will be put off by a shoddy interview. Proper preparation also means less chance of a slip-up, saving you that slow countdown to the end of the new recruit's probation period.

Get the room ready. Book the meeting room and make sure water, hot drinks and enough chairs are available.

Don't discriminate. Avoid questions about race, religion, disability, children and age. Any bias on these grounds and you may be letting the best candidate go. And it's illegal.

Be consistent but flexible. Asking set questions will give candidates a fair chance by giving them equal hurdles to jump. Still, it's important to go off-script to investigate that four-year gap in a CV.

Let them shine. The interviewee should do most of the talking, so make that possible with open questions: 'What is the most difficult decision you've made in your work?' rather than 'Did you like your last job?'

Keep a record. During and after the interview, note down what was said and how you reached your decision. Keep it objective, and don't comment on dress sense or personal hygiene. An unsuccessful candidate complaining to an employment tribunal can ask to see your notes.

Your perfect recruit has signed on the dotted line, and they're working their notice period. Time to think about induction…

CRASH COURSE IN...
EFFECTIVE INDUCTION

Don't wait. As soon as a job offer has been accepted, send the new hire an information pack that includes the company's annual report, staff handbook, newsletters, terms of employment and a guide to their new workplace, so that when they turn up on the first day, they'll already feel some familiarity.

First impressions. Ensure that a colleague is there to meet and greet on the first day. Getting the new person to start half an hour after everyone else on their first day gives you the chance to be ready. Make sure they have a desk – turning up and finding there's nowhere to sit makes them feel unwanted.

What's covered. Your programme should cover basic information such as orientation in the building; where the new person fits into the organisation; health and safety information; and employment terms and conditions.

Tailor it. Some starters will need a specially tailored programme – e.g., school leavers who haven't worked before, people returning to work after a long period away and those with disabilities. You can induct people singly or in groups, or in a combination.

Make it a team effort. The induction process should not be left to one person. The line manager should certainly be involved to welcome the new person to the team and to go through their job description. A senior manager's involvement demonstrates real commitment, but HR should also be there to talk about policies on a range of issues. Above all, don't leave it to a colleague who's not interested.

Learn from the process. There are various ways your organisation can learn from the induction process and from the people you're recruiting. Give new hires a questionnaire after the first few months, or issue them with a little red book so they can write down their observations about the organisation, with the benefit of a fresh pair of eyes.

Do say: 'Great to have you on board. Here's a schedule for the briefings we've lined up today, and an outline of how your induction will progress over the next twelve weeks.'

Don't say: 'Here's your desk, there's the coffee machine, if you've got any questions, save them for the pub quiz on Friday night.'

So, you've safely embedded your new recruit into your team. Before you know it, it's time for someone else's appraisal. Even though you might find it a difficult thing to do, don't stall and don't rush it. This is someone else's career you're dealing with, so treat their appraisal with the respect and seriousness it deserves.

DO IT RIGHT:
THE APPRAISAL

Do it regularly. But twice a year is plenty. An appraisal should simply formalise things you've already talked about. If it throws up any surprises, something's amiss in your day-to-day communication.

Prepare in advance. Don't mutter about hours wasted ticking boxes; show a genuine interest by bringing specific points to discuss. Give your appraisee ample notice too, especially if it's their chance to argue for a pay rise.

Invite their opinions. Ask how they think things are going. This should yield clues as to whether they'll see your analysis as constructive criticism or the spark for a three-day strop.

Be thorough. Build their confidence by highlighting what they're doing right. Aim for more positives than negatives, but be frank about weaknesses.

Be specific. Use examples of clients, jobs or crises to illustrate where change is needed – anything from 'you could have dealt with the Jones account better' to 'how do you think you handled the takeover?'

Complete the loop. A culture of 360-degree feedback can descend into a quagmire of sticky office politics, but providing a formal time to air grievances will ensure that everyone is doing their best to improve things.

Arrive at a conclusion. Set a plan for the future and schedule a further meeting to review progress. Focus on no more than two or three things to improve on, picking the most achievable and crucial to the post.

Even the best manager can't hold on to their best employees for ever. There will come a point when someone will want to say goodbye. But it's not just a case of giving them a nice leaving present – it's the perfect time to ask them for an honest opinion on how they found working with you. Not only will it uncover whatever weaknesses exist in the organisation but you will end the relationship on a good footing.

CRASH COURSE IN...
HANDLING EXIT INTERVIEWS

Publicise it. Telling everybody that you will conduct exit interviews is a positive move. It sends out a clear message to the workforce that you are a listening organisation.

Target all leavers. Don't ignore employees that you are happy to see leaving. There should be no such thing as 'wanted' attrition. Either you chose the wrong person or you've done something to make them not perform. Sometimes, the employee will have been at fault, so it's important to clarify for them what it was they did wrong. Offer refuseniks a questionnaire, or combine the interview with housekeeping tasks such as handing in a laptop and handing out the P45.

Try to keep them. If you want to retain somebody, then act straight away. By their final week, it will be too late to change their mind. Conduct an early meeting to see if they can be turned round, and keep the exit interview separate.

Choose a neutral location. Don't let the line manager do the interview as they may be the problem. It is best done by Human Resources. If the line manager is present, the employee may be reluctant to talk openly.

Set rules of engagement. Make it clear whether the interview is confidential and what will happen to feedback given.

Keep it structured. The objective is to find out why an employee is leaving. Explore their perceptions of the organisation to find the underlying reasons. You can relate what you learn in the exit interview back to the recruitment process, career development, performance measurement and succession planning.

What are they leaving for? It's vital to know where your employee is going: it may be a competitor or a client. And find out what's on offer to them.

Listen, don't react. An exit interview could be an opportunity for an employee to vent their spleen. Remain calm and objective – avoid a slanging match.

Act on the data. Most organisations use the data from exit interviews to look for trends, but there's nothing to stop you taking immediate action if a specific issue is raised.

Do say: 'We'd value feedback on your time here and your reason for leaving.'

Don't say: 'I'm going to give the bugger a good grilling before he collects his P45 and tell him we're glad to see the back of him.'

MEETINGS

'If I had a choice about going to a meeting at a studio or changing a nappy, I'd choose the nappy'
TIM BURTON SAID IT

The bane of many a manager's life, meetings can actually be a positive and useful experience. There's no excuse for time-wasting, boredom or unwanted slanging matches.

Ten Ways to Chair a Meeting

1. Do your homework
2. Write a bullet-proof agenda
3. Stick to it
4. Know who your friends are
5. Pre-empt awkward questions
6. Give everyone a fair shout
7. Keep it moving
8. Have someone take minutes
9. Be clear about the next steps
10. Remember: you're in charge...

THE MANAGEMENT MASTERCLASS

CRASH COURSE IN...
HAVING EFFECTIVE MEETINGS

Is it necessary? You should only hold a meeting when you want people to think together. If you just want to tell them something, you might as well send an e-mail.

Identify the purpose. Meetings should always have a clear, stated objective. That could be making a strategic or operational decision, generating ideas or even raising levels of awareness. The expected outputs should provide an unambiguous focus for the meeting and a measure of its success. Don't hold 'regular' monthly or weekly meetings for their own sake.

Think who should come. Only those critical to the stated objective of the meeting should be there; otherwise, they are wasting the firm's time as well as their own. But if you don't have all the people needed to secure the desired outcome, the meeting will fail, as its results will be open to challenge.

Assign roles. Every successful meeting should have a chair or leader and someone to take minutes. One or more roles are often neglected, with the result that the meeting either lacks direction or concludes with no record of what has been said.

Share it out. Preparation is key, but not just the chair should be involved. If participants are given specific tasks – for example, to lead an item on the agenda – it helps to get their commitment to the meeting. Everyone should share responsibility for the success of the meeting.

Define the process. The word 'agenda' is usually regarded as a list of subject headings, but it should really encapsulate what you're going to do in the meeting. People often focus on the content rather than the process of the meeting. If you're going to brainstorm or give feedback, say so.

Anticipate conflicts. If you know there have been disagreements between some of the participants, prepare in advance. There may have been misunderstandings. It's better to design meetings to address conflicts rather than avoid them; if they get the chance to air their views, they're more likely to buy into the eventual outcome of the meeting.

Keep it tight. Challenge participants if they're deviating from the stated objective of the meeting. Make sure the room is booked immediately after your meeting, so you can't overrun. Think about how much time should be allocated to each agenda item and then halve it.

Do say: 'Forty-five minutes in the boardroom at 1 p.m. on the 17th. I want decisions on x, y and z.'

Don't say: 'I know – let's have a meeting!'

MANAGING WHEN THEY'RE NOT THERE

It's a characteristic of twenty–first–century management that managers will need to manage people who aren't physically in the same office – or country – as them.

CRASH COURSE IN...
MANAGING A VIRTUAL TEAM

Say hello. The most successful virtual teams spend time during their formation period face to face, getting to know each other. It's worth investing in an initial face-to-face meeting, possibly with a facilitator, to foster a social relationship between members and to establish how you'll work together and communicate.

Build trust. Trust is the cement that holds a virtual team together: you can depend on other team members and feel comfortable in opening up to them.

Recruit with care. People who can communicate in the right way at the right time are more likely to be successful in virtual teams. It is vital that a manager has the understanding and awareness of other people's communications preferences.

Don't rely on e-mail. The default communication channel for virtual teams has its shortcomings. The written word is easily misinterpreted. Supplement its use with other forms of communication so that misunderstanding doesn't fester.

Encourage dissent. A healthy organisation needs people to challenge its leaders and each other, but without face-to-face meetings, people become reluctant to speak out. Dissent is one of the greatest assets you can have in a virtual team, because it shows that people have their own opinion and are willing to voice it.

Use technology thoughtfully. Sophisticated tools such as web-chat and collaborative applications like Lotus Notes let people interact around the same documents. But used badly, they can be a disaster. You need to train people to use the technology rather than simply foisting it on them.

Measure outcomes. Performance management is challenging in dispersed teams. You are often giving people a huge degree of spatial and temporal autonomy when you set up a virtual team. So it's best to focus on the outcomes, whether or not they do that through working 9-to-5. Find a personal way to appraise performance, rather than giving feedback via e-mail. And hold regular chats with team members.

Do say: 'By proactively creating virtual teams we can go where the talent is, extend our reach and work more efficiently.'

Don't say: 'We call them a virtual team because they're not quite the real thing.'

If you work in a multinational company or even in a UK firm with offices dotted about the country, it's likely that you will need to work with people operating in different environments from you. You might not even ever get to meet them – so how can you manage them effectively?

DO IT RIGHT:
MANAGE REGIONAL TEAMS

Talk to them. Keep them up-to-date with what's happening across the business. Make sure they hear company info at the right time, through the right channels. Don't rely solely on the intranet – visit them regularly.

Be sensitive. They operate in different markets, and you can't fit a square peg into a round hole. Imposing centrally formulated rules may be unhelpful.

Listen. They're the local experts: where their market is concerned, they may know better than you. Would their know-how work in your other markets? Ask them to present to head office and counterparts in other regions.

Keep an eye on things. Make sure they don't confuse distance with the right to do as they please. It's not the Wild West out there.

Treat them as equals. Give them the same conditions as head-office staff. Working in a far-flung outpost of the empire shouldn't mean shabby offices or fewer benefits. Where benefits aren't transferable, find alternatives.

Involve them. Encourage visits to head office. Include them in central training and introduce them to key people within service departments. Have new staff attend inductions with colleagues from different regions. And invite them to the head office Christmas party.

Spread the love. Encourage staff to apply for positions in other offices. Let them move from region to region, taking their expertise with them. Just make sure that some are happy to choose Bolton over Barcelona.

Okay, so maybe some of your team aren't based in Rio or Rome. They just work from home. Remote working is as everyday in the 2010s as briefcases and braces were in the 1980s.

Masterclass in Remote Working: What is it?

Would Reggie Perrin have cheered up if he hadn't had to perform his daily commute? That's the question devotees of remote working might ask. Spending hours of your life travelling to and from a depressing office is a waste of time and energy, they'll tell you. Especially true if you're a 'knowledge worker' – someone who makes money working with ideas and in so-called creative industries. Do it from home in your pyjamas. That's the remote working dream. NB: Not to be confused with 'not remotely working', which is what many knowledge workers aspire to.

Where did it come from?

Offices and factories grew up as part of the process of industrialisation. But although manufacturers still need the physical presence of their employees (albeit in reduced numbers), it has become clear that service-sector businesses (especially 'knowledge work' businesses) don't have to summon everybody in every day. Work gets done in people's heads and on PCs. Other colleagues can work remotely too. Travelling salespeople have to travel, and may not need a permanent base. Big fat HQs suggest a company that has become complacent and forgotten what business is all about. Hence the move to downsize office buildings and kick people out.

What happens if your staff aren't actually there? It's Monday morning and your department is half-empty. Has swine flu been flying around or is your whole workforce throwing a sickie?

CRASH COURSE IN...
MANAGING ABSENCE

Take control. The first thing you have to do is believe you can control absence. Too many employers have a casual approach towards sickness and absence, opening themselves to abuse.

Write the rules. A policy is essential. When an employee is sick they should ring in themselves, not use their friends and family, and they must talk to a manager. Your policy should also state in what circumstances absence is permissible, expectations about seeking medical help, and what sickness benefit will be paid.

Take a roll call. You can't know whether you have a problem of absenteeism if you aren't recording who's at work and who's not. If employees know that data is being collected, they are less likely to take liberties.

Have a chat. Whether or not you call it a formal back-to-work interview, make sure that you talk to your employee when they return. It's important to establish the reason for their absence, and if it's down to illness, whether it will recur. It's also a good opportunity to update them on what they've missed.

Look for patterns. Look out for suspicious trends in your data. An employee who is regularly off work on Mondays and Fridays is a prime example. Benchmark against competitors and internally to find out if you have a problem and where it is.

Collect the evidence. If you believe an employee is deliberately skiving, you'll need some evidence. Keep records of reasons given for absence when an employee is ill and when they come back, to see if these stack up.

What's behind it. Absenteeism is often a symptom of a deeper malaise. Is your workforce demoralised and poorly motivated? Look for the underlying causes.

THE MANAGEMENT MASTERCLASS

Avoid incentives. Paying people rewards or bonuses for attendance undermines your initiatives to get them to take responsibility for their work. It's also likely to lead to squabbles. Better to offer positive benefits such as flexible working and health benefits that will show that you care about their well-being.

Avoid overkill. Don't encourage your people to come to work when they really are ill. They won't perform, you risk them getting more ill, and they'll spread their germs.

Do say: 'If you're ill, go home and see a doctor; if you're not, be here.'

Don't say: 'I didn't notice you weren't here.'

THE
NUMBERS

MANAGING THE FIGURES

'Please, sir, I want some more'
OLIVER TWIST SAID IT

We all want more wonga. Money – how to get it, manage it, spend it and save it is a critical part of any manager's job. From pleading for more resources to reducing costs, cash is king. And budgets, cash–flow and accounts are things you need to be at ease with – fine if you've studied accountancy, have an MBA or a head for figures. Not so good if you're an 'ideas' or 'people' person. This chapter is all about how to use numbers to get what you want. You don't have to be a pointy-headed maths geek, but figures are the language of business, so you do need to feel at least a little bit comfortable in using them. Here's how to get to grips with the ones and zeros . . .

CASH

'It's clearly a budget. It's got a lot of numbers in it'
GEORGE W. BUSH SAID IT

You've come a long way fast, but you still break out in a nervous sweat come budget time. And the palpitations don't stop there. Keeping the cash flowing over twelve months makes you nauseous; cost-cutting leaves you cold. It's not surprising you feel sick: the numbers speak for themselves — they're the measure on which your performance will be judged. Yet managing money doesn't need to be such an ordeal. With concentration, confidence and an eye for detail, your inner money guru will be released.

CRASH COURSE IN...
SETTING A BUDGET

Don't panic. Setting a budget is not rocket science – it's really just putting numbers to a business plan.

Put strategy first. The plan flows from the strategy, which is broken down into goals and targets for each bit of the organisation. Brainstorm the optimal way to meet your objectives without attaching any pound notes to begin with. If you put the money first, you miss a huge chance for blue-sky thinking.

Forget last year. It might be a useful reference point, but cutting the pie in the same proportions each year is a recipe for maintaining the status quo. You need to be continually questioning the shape of the business.

Devolve and challenge. If you want people to meet their budget, they need to have ownership. Every manager should ask all those who spend money how much they need, and to justify it. You'll end up with budgets that everyone has signed up to.

Raise the bar. Budgets are about setting stretch targets as well as allocating resources. It's down to the judgement of management to reconcile the tension between what's ambitious and what's realistic.

Size doesn't matter. Too often, the bigger your budget, the more important you are. Promote a cultural shift so that brownie points are gained for doing more with less.

Think downside. Risk analysis should go hand-in-hand with budget management. Every department should state the assumptions on which their figures are based, and consider threats and opportunities. The more transparency and clarity there is, the better. Building contingency into the budget is fine, but ensure it's done consistently; don't add a margin at every layer.

Keep on checking. A budget is not to be put away in a drawer for twelve months. Review where you are against the budget as regularly as possible, and take prompt action to reset budgets and reallocate resources when you need to. Effective budget management helps an organisation to meet its strategic objectives without a financial crisis.

Do say: 'Let's look at how we can improve on last year's performance while freeing funding for other parts of the organisation.'

Don't say: 'Anyone in this department who hasn't spent every penny of their budget by 5 April will be shot.'

Whatever budget you're given, it'll never be enough to enable you to do everything you want to. But don't give up at the first hurdle – it's always worth asking for more. That extra cash might get your pet project off the ground or pay for a junior hire that will boost productivity and morale. Remember, never take no for an answer.

Ten Ways to Get a Bigger Budget

1 Fix real problems
2 Link your budget to strategy
3 Demonstrate value for money
4 Give past examples
5 Get real expenditure quotes
6 Test your proposal with your team
7 Benchmark against your competitors
8 Focus on what you can change
9 Give a concise summary
10 Have a back-up plan

CRASH COURSE IN...
BIDDING FOR INTERNAL RESOURCES

Lay the groundwork. Before you put in your bid, you need to achieve as wide a consensus in your favour as possible. Start off by doing a stakeholder analysis to identify the key supporters and blockers. One way to get people on board is to use simple psychology by encouraging them to devise the strategy along with you so they have some ownership.

Pitch it for the audience. When presenting, ensure your message will be well received. Some finance directors will like to see a lot of numbers, others may be receptive to a more intuitive approach.

Be transparent. Your chances of success will be increased by spelling out what benefits will accrue from the level of resource allocated. It's a good idea to present three scenarios. The first might be a low-cost option, the second middle-range, and the third more comprehensive. Start with the base case and then everything else can be analysed in terms of cost benefit.

Keep it internal. Don't start wheeling in customers or management consultants to lobby on your behalf. Your financial director will resent having a gun put to his head. Report their feedback yourself.

Don't make it personal. Once you start undermining your rivals' bids for resources or casting the decision in terms of loyalty, you are politicking and your campaign becomes destructive to the corporate body. And if you threaten to resign unless your bid is granted, you might just have to.

Do say: 'In the following proposal, we have looked at outcomes that would result from varying levels of funding, analysing the benefits for different departments and for the business as a whole.'

Don't say: 'Give me what I'm asking for or you'll regret it.'

Okay, you've got a budget you're reasonably happy with; now you have to make sure it's managed well over the next twelve months. You don't want your income to dry up unexpectedly. Aim for a steady flow, not a flood then a drought.

You have to spend money to make money, so cash-flow management is not about not forking out. It's about keeping your cash-flow in check in a way that allows you to call on funds when you need to make a big spend, but have enough trickling through for day-to-day expenditure.

TEN MUST-KNOW...
CASH-FLOW TIPS

1 **Bill promptly**
It may be all too easy to be distracted by the next job but it's important to issue invoices promptly once work is completed.

2 **Agree terms upfront**
Ideally, you should seek to reach agreement on acceptable payment terms in advance and confirm these in writing to help avoid disputes down the line.

3 **Stalk those payments**
Chase up monies as soon as payment becomes overdue, and even consider sending a reminder two weeks before the official due date. Regular communication with your customers can help avoid problems snowballing.

4   **Offer early-payment incentives**
    Even a discount of 1 or 2 per cent might make all the
    difference. Be sure to distinguish between good and bad
    payers, so you don't give away margin unnecessarily to
    the bad payers. A note of caution: bear in mind that
    some customers are likely to be good payers regardless,
    so offering them a discount may merely fuel more price
    negotiation.

5   **Avoid slow- or non-paying customers**
    Do your homework, particularly with significant
    customers. Ask for and check credit references; contact
    other businesses that have had the same client; consider
    paying for a credit check.

6   **Negotiate payment terms with suppliers**
    Ask your suppliers for extended credit terms: giving
    incentives such as large or regular orders could help. In
    some cases, buying on sale or return may be an option.
    Suppliers could even be open to barter deals, helping
    your business preserve cash.

7   **Schedule payments to suppliers**
    Unless there is a discount for early payment, in general
    you should look to pay suppliers as late as possible.
    Having said that, there may be valued suppliers you want
    to pay earlier for fear that they won't deal with you
    again. Consider arranging a payment schedule that
    eases the strain on your finances so that all bills aren't
    due at once.

8   **Stick to budgets for expenditure**
    Know what you're going to spend on company supplies
    and stick to it. Don't overspend on non-essentials.
    Control overheads, add employees cautiously, and
    make sure staff aren't spending you into difficulties.

9   **Keep prospecting**
    New business development is key to ensure that
    work doesn't dry up. Don't just promote your business
    between jobs. Build effective alliances to leverage
    marketing resources and enhance visibility, and get
    referrals from current clients.

10 **Consider the bigger picture**
    Selling products that lose money will inevitably put a
    strain on cash-flow and so may make no sense. But
    don't rule out selling off a product line or a highly
    profitable part of your business to improve your overall
    financial position.

Masterclass in Credit:
What is it?

'Cash or credit?' asks shopkeeper Bernard Lee in the dour
1965 film of John le Carré's thriller *The Spy Who Came In
From The Cold*. When Richard Burton, playing the spy, is
denied credit, things turn nasty. That's the problem with
credit: we get used to it being there. Those of us who aren't
sitting on piles of cash need it. So do businesses. Few
companies keep much spare cash. Credit fuels investment and
oils the wheels of capitalism. But it depends on having lenders
who are ready to lend. When a credit crunch bites, things get
difficult for everybody.

Where did it come from?

Credit has to do with belief and trust – those are the word's
Latin roots. And moneylenders, of course, go back to Biblical
times. The formal instruments of credit emerged when barter
was no longer a sophisticated enough means of paying for
goods and services. But that's the financial services industry

for you: constantly trying to find new ways of making money. Lending cash has always been, in the best sense of the phrase, a confidence trick. If all depositors chose to withdraw their savings at the same time, we'd get a nasty shock. Not all the money is 'there' – it has been lent elsewhere. No one wants another Northern Rock scenario, with worried savers queuing outside banks. We need to restore credit in credit.

SALES

'The salesman knows nothing of what he is selling save that he is charging a great deal too much for it'
OSCAR WILDE SAID IT

Selling isn't just for the sales team. Sales are the lifeblood of every organisation, whether it's 'selling' direct debit donations if you're a charity or selling double-glazing if you're a window manufacturer. Every manager will be involved in some sort of deal during their career, so it pays to understand how selling and deal-making work, and more importantly, how to be good at it.

Masterclass in Selling:
What is it?

Okay – let's get back to basics. Capitalism is about buying and selling: offering something of value for which a purchaser is prepared to hand over cash, where a genuine choice between alternatives exists. Selling is the core competency for a businessperson. And yet how often do the business media talk about it? Do those of us who are not required to make sales calls look down on 'mere' salespeople?

Where did it come from?

First there was barter. Slapping on a bit of woad, we would meet up outside our caves and swap chickens for sheep, wives for cutting tools, and so on. Then came money. Blame the Romans. The cash value of items was established by the forces of supply, demand and competition. And lo, selling became a central part of commercial life. History does not record when the first ever sales conference took place, but I bet the bar did good business. (You see? We just can't help sneering, can we?) There's more to this than instinct and gut feel – sales is getting technical. Salespeople are made as much as born and you can get better at selling, if you're prepared to try. Smart companies are investing heavily in better data systems, trying to work out who their most valuable customers are and where future sales are likely to come from. Juicy hospitality and

---

WORDS-WORTH:
DEAL

In its origins, the word is about sharing: the same Teutonic root gave us 'dole'. In English, the noun goes back to the ninth century, when a dael was a portion or a part. The verb 'to deal', just as ancient, originally meant to divide up; in card games, it was first used in the sixteenth century. But it's an ambiguous verb. You can 'deal a blow' to someone, and 'dealing with' someone can mean anything from a nice chat to a murder. A deal is a business transaction, though the term, first noted in Canada in the 1830s, was often regarded as slang. In nineteenth-century US usage a 'deal' was something shady or underhand; a 'raw deal' was a swindle. 'Big deal' is a versatile expression, thanks to the Americans, who started using it ironically in the 1950s. Deal or No Deal: big deal.

schmoozing won't work on hard-nosed procurement teams. And when so many products and services have become commoditised, proving the value of your offering is more important than ever.

Of course, increasing your sales is made far easier if you have happy and loyal customers. Keep them sweet, and reap the benefits in future sales.

CRASH COURSE IN...
DEALING WITH FALLING SALES

Be positive. The first thing you've got to do is have some self-belief. If you have your head down, you won't sell anything.

Don't stop marketing. There's plenty of evidence to show that firms that cut their advertising and marketing budgets lose out in the short term as well as in the long run. Instead of cutting activity, consider diverting spend to more accountable forms of marketing, such as the web, direct response or promotions.

Target your effort. In hard times, people put a lot of effort into chasing every opportunity they think they can get, and as a result, they half-sell to twice as many customers. Identify your best customers and concentrate your effort on them.

Sharpen up your sales team. In boom times, sales teams are lazy and don't work as hard as they can. In tough times, you need to manage them effectively. Cut out the dead wood and make sure you retain your stars. Provide training if needed, and use proficiency tests, references and psychometric testing to ensure those you recruit have the right stuff.

Incentivise your people to sell. Make sure everyone in the firm appreciates the importance of selling, and introduce incentives for those who refer leads to the sales team.

Mind who you sell to. Switch off supply rather than continue to feed a customer who is a late payer. Link sales commissions to cash, so the sales force sells only to people who pay.

Do say: 'We are going to sell our way through this.'

Don't say: 'It's hopeless.'

Ten Ways to Win a Contract

1   Get on the pitch list
2   Ask detailed questions about the brief
3   Understand the purchasing process
4   Understand the purchasing people
5   Know what the competition offers
6   Have beautifully prepared examples of your work
7   Coach your references on how to sell you
8   Don't miss deadlines
9   Rehearse your presentation
10 Rigorously detail and justify your costs

THE MANAGEMENT MASTERCLASS

CRASH COURSE IN...
CUSTOMER LOYALTY

Why loyalty matters. It's cost-effective to look for sales from your existing customers – when tempting offers from competitors abound, the goodwill you've built up can make all the difference.

Collect the data. You need to know who your customers are before you build your relationship with them. Are you collecting customer data? Storing transactional data? Trying to influence your customers' behaviour without any data is like driving in the fog without headlights.

Segment your customers. The old adage is that 20 per cent of your customers account for 80 per cent of your revenue. You need to identify who your most profitable customers are and which ones you're likely to influence through your marketing and communication. Your objective should be to treat different customers differently. If regular customers are beneficial to you, you want to identify potential regular customers and target them with relevant offers.

Use your web presence. Loyal and frequent customers will look to your website, so make the most of it. Websites and e-mail offer an extremely cheap channel to talk to your customers.

Reappraise your products. Find out which products your most profitable customers are buying – that may lead you to rationalise your product line.

Treat your customers right. Research identifies key factors that companies must address: delivering on promises; being honest and open with customers; and being relevant to them. Otherwise, your offers will fall on deaf ears.

Make them feel special. All loyalty marketing is about recognition through offering some form of privilege valued by the customer. That could be points rewards, an invitation to early store openings, or access to a VIP lounge.

Appeal to thrift. Customers who are struggling to survive won't be lured by discounts on luxury hotels or accessories. So make sure there's an alternative that offers them the chance to really save money.

Do say: 'We value your custom. Here's a thank you.'

Don't say: 'Sorry, dear, that offer's for new customers only.'

COSTS

You can have the best sales team in the world but if you're haemorrhaging money, paying bloated salaries or wasting revenue on unnecessary products and services, you're still going to be in the red at the end of every month. But embarking on a cost-cutting bonanza isn't the panacea for all your financial ills. If done incautiously or with too much fervour, it can cause great damage. Cut costs, but cut costs intelligently.

Don't you believe it... Cutting costs boosts profits

Here are two common profitability problems that won't be fixed by cost-cutting:

Fudged pricing strategy. In any market, some customers will pay extra for value, while others will just want the lowest price. You can't satisfy both. Either your costs are too high to make money in the second segment, or you aren't spending enough to provide the value that the first one expects. While markets were buoyant, you probably got away with this, but when it gets tough, it's decision time. Either organise everything you do to be the lowest-cost producer, becoming the Ryanair of your industry, or spend money on differentiating yourself and go for the added-value approach.

Unprofitable customers or products. This is more common than you'd think; in cases like these, reducing costs won't help. You have to roll up your sleeves and get into the detail. It's not enough to look at average margins – they can hide a multitude of sins. Look instead at profitability across individual lines and businesses.

Masterclass in Cost Reduction:
What is it?

When boom turns to bust, it becomes necessary to relearn a few basic principles that may have gone out of fashion. Keeping costs down, for example. We all know what happens when things are going well. A hiring spree. Business–class flights. Nice hotels. Celebratory meals in top restaurants.

Lavish corporate sponsorship of events. In a downturn? Belts are tightened. And most items listed above disappear.

Where did it come from?

Cost reduction is where management consultancy came in. Accountants rebranded themselves in the pre-war years, putting a focus on 'cost accounting', which they offered as a consultancy service. The forgotten art of 'time and motion studies' was also about the costs of doing business. And venerable old firms make no bones about their core purpose of finding efficiency savings and cost reductions. During a cost-reduction phase, some businesses are forced to take a 'blank sheet of paper' approach and re-engineer their entire cost base. Downturns are a time when tough and unpleasant decisions on costs can no longer be put off. So suppliers will have to look out as buyers cast an ever more sceptical eye on the prices being charged. And if any lower-cost alternative providers are setting up here or abroad, watch out. They may just be about to eat your lunch.

TEN WAYS TO...
CUT YOUR COSTS BY 20 PER CENT

1 **Create a cost-conscious workplace culture**
Develop a culture where everybody is responsible for challenging costs, from the receptionist to senior management. Celebrate cost reductions as you do business wins. It is vital to start caring about cost management before the situation becomes critical and hasty decisions are made.

2 **Lead by example**

Leaders need to set an example by demonstrating to employees that they care about saving money, even on the smallest items. Don't book the most expensive hotels when you are asking your own management teams to take the budget option.

3 **Keep the green light flashing**

Instil a sense of urgency, so employees act immediately to reduce costs and maximise profitability. If it does not remain high on the boardroom agenda, employees will see the directors' crusades as 'the flavour of the month', and the drive to cut costs will fall to the bottom of everyone's in-tray.

4 **Establish what your costs really are**

You may believe your costs are under control, but your perceived 'watertight ship' may not be as leak-proof as you thought. Forensically examine and benchmark your costs line by line.

5 **Be market-wise**

It is critical that you are aware of the constantly changing supplier market for your costs so you can identify developments that you can capitalise on. By enhancing your knowledge, you will have more confidence to use one supplier for a number of items, and thus benefit from a 'basket' cost rate.

6 **Don't purchase things you don't need**

Buy what you need, not what your suppliers would like to sell you. Many suppliers make much more money from supplementary services or add-ons like service or maintenance agreements.

7 **Let suppliers know about your cost review**
Also refuse to accept price increases unchallenged or any suggestion from your suppliers that 'our prices are higher because we provide superior quality and service' or 'our prices cannot be beaten'. During negotiations, present the value of your business to the supplier.

8 **Establish key supplier performance**
Make sure you obtain management information from suppliers relating to any cost increases/decreases, otherwise these could easily be hidden in an invoice incorporating a large number of supplied items. Constantly monitor their performance levels and adherence to your contract.

9 **Jettison suppliers only as a last resort**
Reducing costs is not just about going to a cheaper supplier. Good relationships in any line of business are fundamental; the one with your supplier is no exception.

10 **Create a long-term cost-management programme**
Potential savings are great but they don't mean anything unless they are realised. After implementing a culture of cost-consciousness, appoint cost champions to drive the programme forward. Constantly monitor the situation to ensure that staff are not slipping into old habits; that suppliers are charging correct prices; and that service standards match the agreed specification.

PAY

'It's all about the bucks, kid, the rest is
conversation'
GORDON GEKKO SAID IT

Pay, remuneration, emoluments – whatever you want to call
a salary – it can be a headache for the novice manager,
whether negotiating with staff or asking for your own pay
rise. Not only is pay an emotive subject, but it can also be
mysterious, guarded by people who think they're paid more
than others, or deliberately shrouded in secrecy by managers
who want to get away with paying the least possible.

Masterclass in Remuneration:
What is it?

Hard pay. Money. Wonga. So vulgar, these terms. How much
better to draw a veil over the crude reality of the 'cash nexus'
and use the most polysyllabic term we can think of. As usual,
Shakespeare was on to the absurdity of this word 400 years
ago. The clown Costard in *Love's Labour's Lost* is handed a
payment by a nobleman (described as a 'remuneration') and
inspects his winnings: 'Now will I look to his remuneration.
Remuneration! O, that's the Latin word for three farthings:
three farthings, remuneration . . . Remuneration! Why, it is a
fairer name than French crown. I will never buy and sell out
of this word.'

Where did it come from?

Its Latin roots imply paying someone back for something – a
recompense (hence 'compensation'). At the heart of capitalist
exchange is the notion of fair play and indeed fair pay. Trade
is all about getting something for something. So when

somebody's remuneration gets out of hand, the receivers of said excessive remuneration are in a sense offending against the very spirit of business itself. They also arouse suspicion by using such a fancy term to refer to what, in plain language, simply means great wads of cash. Top people's pay, which is what most people think of when they hear the word 'remuneration', has got wildly out of hand in recent years. Since the early 1990s, chief executives, financiers and others have been trying to outdo each other in the sprint to get their snouts into the trough first. Where once a CEO might have expected to get paid 15 or 20 times what the most junior employee received, that ratio has now soared to 200, 300 and even 400 times. We simply cannot go on like this. Can we?

Pay is often complicated by the fact that many people have a salary but work in a bonus system where the bonus can often be greater than the basic salary. Used as an incentive, it always had the potential to backfire spectacularly.

THE MANAGEMENT MASTERCLASS

WORDS-WORTH: BONUS

A bonus is a good thing – or meant to be, etymologically speaking, at least. The word is Latin, though not correct Latin: the word for 'good thing' is not bonus but bonum, *which also means wealth, benefit, profit, etc. The mistake was made in the late eighteenth century, when the word bonus first appeared, probably in Stock Exchange slang. Bonus is better translated as 'good man'. Good men receive bonuses, defined as payments over and above what is due to them as their normal remuneration, but so do lots of others. This is the source of much of the controversy surrounding bonuses. In common parlance, a bonus is a reward for exceptional performance or a way of distributing surplus profits. But among many potential recipients, bonuses are something to which they are entitled, losses and government bailouts notwithstanding. The difference between these two interpretations goes some way towards explaining the sense of grievance felt on both sides and why, good thing or not, 'bonus' has become a dirty word.*

Masterclass in Performance-related Pay: What is it?

If only we could get what we paid for. This is the management dream that lies behind PRP. Why not reward an individual's performance according to his or her direct output? This should provide a clear incentive for staff to work harder and produce more. But life does not work like that. For most people, money is more of a 'hygiene factor' than a true provider of inspiration. Except in the purest of sales-driven environments, performance rewards don't always motivate people to work harder. Basic pay is what counts, what gets people to turn up. And a bonus is just that – a bonus.

Where did it come from?

'Piecework' is the purest form of PRP – no-one gets paid until something gets made. The origins of piecework are pre-industrial, but it was a concept picked up by Frederick Winslow Taylor early last century in his theory of 'scientific management'. The business world turned deeply sceptical just as governments of both colours decided that PRP is what the public sector needed to drive through change. But it is getting harder to find anyone with a good word to say for it. In the City, bankers love their bonuses, as do senior execs at top corporations. But bonuses distort behaviour and set team members against each other. And why should the CEO take credit for the work everybody else has done? PRP has simply not… performed.

Knowing how to get what you're worth is an essential skill worth having. Not only does it prove that you know how to negotiate successfully but it also shows you know your market value. Never pass up an opportunity to ask for more.

YOUR ROUTE TO THE TOP...
HOW TO GET A PAY RISE

Know your worth. Understand not just your value in the market, but also the value of your job in the marketplace – there is a difference.

Know what your walk-away position is. Create a strong alternative in your mind. You are much more likely to negotiate confidently if you have something else up your sleeve.

Get to know your boss. Remember: building a relationship with them is like running a marathon, not a short sprint. Drip, drip, drip over time.

Cultivate allies. Changes to pay are rarely just down to your immediate superior. Think of the mood that surrounds the decision-makers. Who else has influence? What do they think you are worth?

Choose your moment. Make sure your boss is in the right mindset – don't approach them just before they start presenting to the board or heading off on holiday. Make sure they are able to give the matter the attention it needs.

Decide what to compromise on. What are you willing to accept? The negotiation is not just about the pay. You need to consider the benefits, responsibilities and hours too.

If you get knocked back, ask questions. Work together on the criteria you must meet to merit a pay rise. This will give you a clear focus. Can you show you are delivering on this?

Stay positive. If it doesn't go the way you planned, focus on the future.

THE
CHALLENGES

COMMON PROBLEMS

'A problem is a chance to do your best'
DUKE ELLINGTON SAID IT

As a manager, you will spend most of your time dealing with people – and people defy logic. How many times has a boss or a colleague surprised you with their unexpected behaviour? Humans are unpredictable, unreliable and fallible. They are also brilliant, loyal and tough. It is far better to accept that your team won't always behave how you expect them to, than to convince yourself into thinking that they are programmable automatons. So embrace the messy human chaos, and learn to think on your feet. Expect – even look forward to the fact – that each day will bring an invigorating set of new problems to fix. View them as opportunities for you and your team to exercise creativity, intelligence and original thinking to solve them. A great boss gives employees the power and freedom to solve their own problems but will quickly and decisively take control should a situation demand.

There are two types of management challenges that you will be presented with: the common problems and the crises. The skills you hone while solving the smaller problems will stand you in good stead for dealing with the biggies.

PEOPLE PROBLEMS

It's naïve to think that you will get on with everyone at work all of the time – or get on with them at all. Work isn't a popularity contest and you will inevitably come into contact with difficult people. You might even find one on your team. Bores, egotists, gossips, bullies and incompetents will sooner or later cross your path. What to do?

YOUR ROUTE TO THE TOP...
HOW TO HANDLE TRICKY PEOPLE

Get to the heart. Whether it's a colleague, client or boss, it's better to try to understand tricky people than to avoid them. Work out how they see things and then find a way to work comfortably with them.

Control the control freak. If your boss is the anxious type, pre-empt their concerns. To stop them jumping in as your finger reaches for the send button, share your ideas upfront.

Don't get dumped on. If your manager tends to deliver 'top priority' tasks for 'urgent' projects and then disappear, help them to focus. Ask them to describe their ideal result: what, when and how do they want it? By forcing them to think it through, you'll avoid unreasonable last-minute changes.

Silence the sceptic. When presenting a new plan, ask questions to understand what makes the doubters tick. Listen carefully. Identify the root of their problem and you can address their real concerns.

Calm the stress cadet. If your colleague is in regular meltdown, concentrate their attention on what can be done here and now. Battling a presentation, pitch and project work? Small steps will lead to significant results.

Resist charmers. Don't get taken in by empty, eloquent flair. Ask tough questions to keep them on track. Try: 'What does that mean in practice?' Help them distinguish between dreams and reality and you'll get the best of both.

A difficult person can really affect the atmosphere of a place. And a negative atmosphere saps energy, exacerbates existing problems and lowers morale. Galling though this situation might first appear, it is important to nip it in the bud before discontent takes hold.

Ten Ways to Combat Negativity

1 Spot what's wrong and change it early
2 Be there as a sounding-board
3 Respond to people's concerns
4 Lead with trust, not rules
5 Be consistent
6 Show people the effects of their griping
7 Involve moaners in solutions
8 Challenge untruths
9 Focus on people's positive points
10 Don't take it personally

Ever dreaded having to speak to someone about something unpleasant? It takes courage to broach a difficult topic with either a boss or someone you manage. It's easy to put a difficult conversation off, kidding yourself that the problem will magically go away by itself. There's never going to be a 'right time', so go on – just bite the bullet.

YOUR ROUTE TO THE TOP...
HOW TO HAVE DIFFICULT CONVERSATIONS

Get ready. Prevent difficult conversations from becoming emotionally charged. Ask yourself 'What do I want to achieve here?' before you go into the conversation. The answer can act as a reminder to pull back from an argumentative stance.

Start with the facts. Sharing your feelings is a powerful way to express why something is important to you, but differentiate between facts (the report has three errors in it), assumptions (it was clearly done at the last minute) and emotions (I feel let down). Facts are indisputable, so are easier to share first.

Describe actual behaviours. If delivering constructive criticism, avoid the infamous 'feedback sandwich' (good-bad-good). It comes across as disingenuous and dilutes the impact of your message.

Allow time for reflection. Give people the chance to respond, but don't force them: arrange to talk about it later.

Open up. Listen without showing any negative or defensive emotions (this will be difficult but is essential). Show that you understand not only what they are saying but how they feel.

Collaborate. When asked about the turning point in the Cold War, Soviet leader Gorbachev replied that the crucial moment came at the 1986 Reykjavik summit with US President Reagan. This was the first time the leaders had entered into genuine dialogue, sharing their values, assumptions and aspirations. Their resulting trust and understanding began to reverse the nuclear arms race. Ask questions and work together without judgement.

Keep moving. If you can't agree on an issue, don't waste hours debating it. This conflict quicksand will get you nowhere. Park the issue and move on – you can always come back to it.

There will be many occasions when your only option is to say 'no' to someone. First-time managers can find this difficult because they don't want to be a naysayer or they are too scared to assert themselves. But learning how to say no clearly and effectively is a necessary skill that only gets easier with practice.

Ten Ways to Say No

1 Start by saying no
2 Practice makes perfect
3 Give your reasons
4 Keep your message clear
5 Ask questions
6 Acknowledge their situation...
7 ... but stick to your guns
8 Reassure them
9 Own up to unrealistic expectations
10 Offer constructive options

WORK PROBLEMS

If it's not people who present you with challenges, it'll be the work itself. Whether you're being assailed by customer complaints or faced with a particularly difficult decision, it's your job to take control and show who's boss.

Ten Ways to Make a Tough Decision

1 Take time out
2 Think: is it right for the company?
3 Consider those who'll be affected
4 Believe in yourself
5 Do your research
6 Focus
7 Stick to your guns
8 Be prepared for fallout
9 Remember: it can only make you stronger
10 Don't repeat your mistakes

YOUR ROUTE TO THE TOP...
FACE A PREDICAMENT

Acknowledge your strengths. Have you been here before? You've probably dealt with something similar, perhaps even worse. Remembering how you coped in the past will give you the confidence to do it again.

Let off steam. Take time to vent. Find a supportive friend or trusted colleague and get it off your chest. Once you're done you will feel stronger and ready for action.

Identify the problem. Hunt down the root cause of your feelings and deal with it. Don't fight unnecessary battles.

Get it down on paper. When we are at boiling point, we can be flooded by emotion. Writing about how you feel is a cathartic exercise and will help you get things in perspective.

Stop worrying. Decide what you can do about the situation you're in and what is outside your control. Focus on areas you can influence and come to terms with the rest.

Take the long-term view. Remember that nothing lasts for ever. If you keep reminding yourself that the current situation will certainly come to an end, you will be less likely to do something rash and reckless.

Take small steps. If you can't see the route to resolution, break it down and tackle it one small step at a time. Keep going and the solution will eventually emerge.

Make a decision and get on with it. If you take action it will distract you from worrying, create a sense of progress towards resolving the crisis and help you feel in control – all of which will lead to increased calmness.

Okay, so you've got to grips with making tough decisions. But what if you come under attack for the decision you ended up making? Or what if you arrive at work one day and face a disgruntled client? Or even worse, a senior manager who's after your scalp for a departmental cock-up? It's at times like these that your toughness will be tested, but don't think you have to be like Rambo, defending yourself with all guns blazing. Be assertive, not aggressive; measured, not impulsive.

Ten Ways to Deal with Flak

1 Don't take it personally . . .
2 . . . but do take stock: are the jibes fair?
3 Act on them only if they are
4 Don't rush to respond
5 Use it as a chance to think about your strengths
   and weaknesses
6 Change what doesn't work
7 Celebrate what does
8 Thank the critic for helping you
9 Learn the lesson
10 Move on

MIND YOUR MANNERS:
HANDLING COMPLAINTS

Put yourself in the customer's shoes. No matter how trivial or unbelievable a complaint seems, offer the attention you'd expect yourself.

Don't tell your staff that a customer is 'moaning'. It doesn't pay to be disrespectful.

Log it. Keep a record, not just a Post-It. The business looks bad if someone follows up a complaint and you have no idea what they're referring to.

Speak to them. If they have written in, ring them back. It's much easier to build up trust if there's human interaction, and the customer will know that you are on the case.

Deal with it. Don't put a problem to one side and hope it will go away. Looking into complaints may not be the fun part of your job, but delays will just make the situation worse.

Give a timescale. It's much more reassuring and professional for the customer to know exactly when you will get in touch. 'Later this afternoon' will sound like you're trying to fob them off.

Be fair. Make sure employees aren't just made scapegoats for misunderstandings. Launching into a tirade against a junior member of staff to save face will make everyone hate you.

Complaints always arise. With all the care and attention in the world things can still go wrong. But if the same complaints keep coming in, warning bells should ring. How a business responds reveals its character.

Much of modern management centres on project work. Despite the best will in the world, there will be occasions when a project will wobble – time for you to don your Superman cloak and stage a rescue. Ker-pow!

CRASH COURSE IN...
PROJECT RECOVERY

Admit you're in trouble. As with alcoholics, the first step is to acknowledge you have a problem. Look for early warning signs, which include stakeholders who are not engaged, lack of clarity, things that haven't happened.

Don't look back. Concentrate on plotting the direction forward, not a lengthy post mortem. It's more important to stop failing and stabilise.

Call in consultants. Some consultancies have specialist project recovery teams who have long experience, but it's much more expensive when things go wrong than calling them in when you are designing the project at the beginning.

Don't point the finger. Laying blame won't help you recover. People will give you warning of further problems only if there is a no-blame culture.

Consider cancellation. This may be the best option if your project is not going to deliver the functionality promised, will cost more than the forecast return on investment, or will finish too late to meet a market opportunity. With large projects, conduct a gateway review before each new stage of commitment.

Give and take. Among your options to recover a project are: reduce its scope or specification (but only if it still meets its business objectives), add extra resources or extend deadlines. One option might be to stagger the handover so that you don't need everything finished at the same time.

Rewrite contracts. This may be the time to renegotiate contracts, including performance incentives with suppliers and even your own people.

Inject fresh blood. Sacking the entire team might be inadvisable, but new people will bring fresh ideas with no emotional baggage. The optimum is a mix of old and new blood.

Rally the troops. Restoring team morale is a priority and there are a number of ways you can do this. Chalk up some easy wins, celebrate successes, and get the sponsors of the project to come and show their appreciation. Give everyone a couple of days off.

Do say: 'At this early stage we are reviewing the resources, timescales and budgets to ensure the project's successful completion.'

Don't say: 'If we just carry on, perhaps it will sort itself out.'

These scenarios can make your team feel very stressed. You've just asked one of your teams to carry out a simple little task; one team member did an impression of the Large Hadron Collider and another burst into tears. Quite a few of your people have been looking like they're close to breaking point…

CRASH COURSE IN...
MANAGING STRESS

Understand what it is. It's important to appreciate the difference between stress and pressure. We all thrive on pressure; but only when the individual becomes unable to cope does it become stress. That's when someone is no longer in personal control and feels there is no way of regaining it.

Spell it out. A written policy should tell your people what to do if they become stressed in the course of their work, and what responsibility you'll take as employer. Under the Health and Safety at Work Act 1974, you must take measures to control the risk. Failure to do so could cost you dear in an employment tribunal.

Check the sick roll. A spike in sickness or absentee days is often the first indicator of stress in one part of the organisation.

Get the measure of it. Call it a stress audit or risk assessment, but you must find out who is feeling stressed and whether they are clustered in a particular area. If you have more than five employees, health and safety regulations require you to assess the risk.

Identify the causes. Among the common causes of stress are: excessive workload; an individual's lack of control over their work; poor relationship with boss; poor work/life balance; and an emphasis on fault-finding rather than encouragement. Bullying and organisational change are two more.

Blame the management. The biggest single source of stress is incompetent, poorly trained and inappropriately promoted managers – don't be one of them. Get training.

Be attentive. Quick-fix managers may spot a problem, but they simply refer it on to someone else, such as occupational health. Good managers intervene, to establish trust and commitment.

Do say: 'People who suffer from stress are not going to perform at their best for us.'

Don't say: 'If you can't stand the heat, get out of the bloody kitchen.'

No manager is infallible, even if they are convinced that they are master or mistress of the universe. Humility doesn't cost anything but hubris certainly does. Face the facts. You are going to make mistakes, take wrong decisions and back the wrong people. Failure is par for the course and gives you valuable experience, but don't succumb to self-pity – it's weak and indulgent. It's better instead to pick yourself up, dust yourself off and face the next challenge with courage.

'Success is the ability to go from one failure to another with no loss of enthusiasm'
WINSTON CHURCHILL SAID IT

How to flop with flair

- Fail with a bang, not a whimper. If you make enough noise, people will remember you.
- Reflect on and learn from your disaster.
- Don't let one flop stop you from trying again. Failing doesn't make you a failure.
- Flaunt your scars. They make you more marketable.

Ten Ways to Recover from a Fall

1 Get straight back in the saddle
2 Stay visible
3 Be open about your mistake
4 Remember, everyone fails at some point
5 Learn from the experience
6 Don't dwell on it
7 Believe in yourself
8 Use it as a catalyst for change
9 Prove your strength
10 Don't be frightened to fail again

WHEN THE SHIT HITS THE FAN

'Any idiot can face a crisis – it's day to day living that wears you out'
ANTON CHEKOV SAID IT

One day it's business as usual, the next day you are in the midst of a disaster. The media is ready to crucify you, and your company's very future is in doubt. Your immediate reaction might be to run for the hills, but panicking won't get you anywhere. A sudden crisis is a chance for you to shine, so take a deep breath, sit down and stay focused. You *can* get through a challenging situation, whether it's the recession, making redundancies or dealing with a PR disaster.

CRISES

It's 8.30 a.m. You're in a great mood as you arrive at your desk. Then, bam! An e-mail from the boss demanding you meet her in her office immediately…

CRASH COURSE IN...
MANAGING A CRISIS

Expect the worst. Plan ahead for a crisis. You need a business continuity plan to keep operations going in the event of a warehouse fire, systems failure or any other disaster. You should also have a communications plan that outlines how you will communicate quickly and effectively with key stakeholders such as customers, suppliers, shareholders and the media. Make it clear who has specific responsibility for contacting particular individuals, and how other groups will be contacted.

Stay cool. In practice, most crisis-hit executives run round like headless chickens. You need to take a cool strategic over-view. Ask yourself if everyone has a common view of the situation. How bad can it get? What message do you need to put out and how? The first twenty-four hours are often crucial.

How do others see it? What counts are other people's perceptions, not your own. To you, it might be a storm in a teacup, but if your customers, investors or other audiences perceive the situation to be damaging, that's what you must address.

Get the media on your side. Hold a press conference or issue a statement, and give journalists maximum access – they can be your best ally. But if they believe that you are slow in providing information, they will lose confidence.

Beware of crisis creep. Watch for warning signs. A story that features repeatedly in the trade press will soon be picked up by the national media.

Tell the truth. You may not be able to tell everything you know – for example, if an issue is sub judice, or the Stock Exchange needs to be informed – but at least try to explain why you can't tell all.

Say sorry. An apology usually helps to diffuse the situation. You may not wish to admit liability but express your regret that it occurred and your determination to prevent it happening again.

Take personal control. Don't try and hide behind spin doctors or consultants. Use them, but make sure that you are the spokesperson.

Be human. Crisis management isn't a black art. If you behave as a human being, you can't go far wrong.

Do say: 'We would like to express our deepest sympathies to those who have been affected, and shall leave no stone unturned in our efforts to establish exactly how this happened.'

Don't say: 'Crisis? What crisis? Let's just keep our heads down, chaps, and in a week's time it will have blown over.'

History lessons: Patience in adversity

When he headed to Zaire in 1974 for the Rumble in the Jungle against title-holder George Foreman, no one gave Muhammad Ali a chance. His opponent was an unbeaten bruiser seven years his junior who had won thirty-seven of his forty fights through knockouts, most of them inside three rounds. Ali understood his physical disadvantage and ditched the fancy footwork, instead targeting Foreman's one untested quality – stamina. His 'rope-a-dope' ploy involved lying on the ropes and dodging the blows that rained on him. Ali seemed to be taking a hiding, but he was dictating the fight, goading Foreman and moving his head swiftly to minimise the impact of his blows. After eight rounds, tiredness and the African heat took its toll on the now desperate Foreman. Ali seized his chance and laid him out. Try exercising some Ali-style patience and pick your moment to unleash your attack. That one-two combination of fox-like cunning and muscle will send your rivals reeling.

If a crisis does kick off and senior management decide to keep it under wraps for a while, don't fall into the trap of thinking that as long as you keep *schtum*, nothing will leak out. Your colleagues aren't stupid. Sudden meetings, pensive faces and weekends spent in the office will raise their suspicions, and the rumour mill will quickly spring into action. It doesn't take long for misinformation to quickly become fact, and for small things to be blown out of all proportion. Before you know it, you've got a situation on your hands.

Ten Ways to Handle Rumours

1 Face it, tongues will always wag
2 Be open about what's going on
3 Be firm when bearing bad news
4 Address individuals' concerns
5 Build a trusting atmosphere
6 Promote intranet discussion
7 Trust your own judgement
8 Nip trouble in the bud
9 Tell the truth
10 Don't fudge the issue

Unfortunately, Lady Luck can play her part in upsetting our well-constructed plans – we are all exposed to the vagaries of boom and bust. Coping with a recession will test your management skills to the core, so it's important to know what you're up against.

CRASH COURSE IN...
COMMUNICATING IN TOUGH TIMES

Talk more, not less. In uncertain times, staff need more information. If there are long silences, they'll come to their own conclusions, so ensure there are frequent opportunities to communicate with staff and receive feedback. Other stakeholders will be hungry for information to evaluate any risks they may be exposed to.

Be consistent. Discrepancies between what you tell the outside world and your own people may cause resentment, especially if you lay off staff and make cutbacks.

Tell it like it is. The priority of your people has become survival, so there is little appetite for the more luxurious features of internal comms, such as self-development or feeding their artistic soul. They're concerned with jobs and security, and they want the facts.

Remember to listen. Communication is a two-way street. You may not have all the answers. It takes courage, but you need to listen to people's questions, and then go off and see if you can find the answers. In a booming market, you may get away with simply broadcasting what you want people to hear; in a recession, it's vital to understand what they're thinking.

Choose the right channel. For internal communications, face-to-face interaction becomes far more important in recessionary times. Supervisors and line managers can play an important role here. Data suggests that employees have greater trust in their immediate line manager than those higher up the organisation.

Get the web covered. All big brands in the news need a social media engagement programme during a recession, for two reasons: first, to counter or correct criticism, and second, to drive people to their own, relevant, website content.

Spread the word. Whoever you're talking to, don't forget to spread the good news when there's some to talk about. It will raise morale, show people the way forward and create a sense of buzz in your organisation.

Do say: 'We'd like to keep you informed about how we're facing up to this difficult situation – and hear about the issues that concern you.'

Don't say: 'We've got nothing to say – and that's off the record.'

WORDS-WORTH: RECESSION

For a while, 'recession' was the word that dared not speak its name. Such is its mystical power that it was thought that merely saying the R-word out loud would bring a sharp decline in economic activity. Strictly, it means an economic decline marked by two successive quarters of negative growth in gross domestic product. The word comes from the Latin verb recedere, *'to withdraw'. 'Recession' is the act of receding, withdrawing or retreating. Newspapers talked of recessions in output, stock prices and so on throughout the twentieth century, but the modern sense, of a decline in a whole economy, is recorded first in an* Economist *article published just days after the 1929 Wall Street crash. It said an industrial recovery wouldn't be long in coming, 'even if we have to face an immediate recession of some magnitude'. Then it was a euphemism, used in place of scarier words like 'crash', 'slump' or 'panic'. But no one was fooled. In due course, new euphemisms arrived – 'period of adjustment', anyone? – while 'recession' became as scary as those other words...*

REDUNDANCY

Making someone redundant is the worst case scenario for every manager but it's also a chance to prove your professionalism. The best managers will try to limit the damage as much as possible – it always pays to think ahead …

CRASH COURSE IN...
AVOIDING REDUNDANCY

Plan ahead. Try to envisage what talent you will need in five or ten years' time. Workforce planning in sectors such as manufacturing allows you to plan ahead for a temporary downturn in production. Offering fixed-term contracts where appropriate can also obviate the need to make redundancies.

Stop hiring. There's a lot of movement in the job market, so you can achieve a certain amount of saving through natural wastage. However, clearly, you need to have people in the right jobs, so you will have to continue some recruitment.

Cut overtime. If you're in a sector where people are still paid overtime, look at reducing or scrapping it altogether to cut the wage bill.

Target temps. Agency and other temporary staff are usually taken on as a lining for the fatter times. If you want to keep your permanent, skilled people, look at cuts in the temporary part of the workforce first.

Look for volunteers. Offering voluntary redundancy should be standard practice, but act with caution. If it's offered across the board, your more valuable people are often the confident ones who go out and find a new job; therefore make sure you have had effective career conversations so they know their value to the firm. Make it clear you will have final say on who goes.

Discuss it. If you're laying off more than twenty people, there's a statutory obligation to consult with employees' representatives. But approach it as a genuine attempt to find out whether your people can come up with ideas to avoid redundancies.

Redeploy. Part of your business may be faltering while another is still growing. There's a need for joined-up deployment. Using existing employees can save on redundancy costs and recruitment costs – you have somebody who understands the culture of the business.

Take a break. If you judge the downturn to be temporary, offer sabbaticals, extended training or study leave as ways to cut the wage bill while keeping the door open for individuals to return when business improves.

Do say: 'At this difficult time, we are going to explore as many options as we can to avoid making redundancies.'

Don't say: 'We're all doomed!'

You've done your best to avoid making redundancies but the inevitable has happened. Now it's your turn to deliver the news.

CRASH COURSE IN...
HANDLING LAY-OFFS

It's not about slackers. When you announce redundancies, make it clear that it's not personal. Redundancy occurs when there is a cessation of business or a reduction of work; you have to assure people that it's not a reflection on them as an individual, but rather on their position.

Let the people speak. If more than twenty are being made redundant in a ninety-day period, you must consult the trade union or an employees' representative. Remember, it's a consultation, not a negotiation, but you must be able to show that you have considered what they said in good faith.

Be selective. Draw up selection criteria that reflect the attributes, skills and experience you will need in your organisation. Score all those in the frame against these criteria and, hey presto, the choice is made.

Discriminate at your peril. Your selection process must ensure that no one is more likely to be chosen for redundancy because of their gender, race, disabilities, sexual orientation or age. Discrimination is a far more serious issue than unfair dismissal.

Do you really want volunteers? Offering voluntary redundancy is a nice idea, but you could end up losing the people you want to keep. And will they be disaffected if they apply and are turned down?

Manage the bad news. Make sure you tell people individually, face to face, and plan to ensure that all those concerned will be available at the right time. Text message and e-mail must be avoided at all costs.

Do the right thing. Be generous; don't just give the legal minimum pay-off, but offer those you're dispensing with support, and help them to find new work. You can ask people to waive their rights in return for more generous redundancy terms. The other reason is to be seen as reasonable and fair by those who stay.

Cuddle the survivors. Make sure they understand what your strategy for the future is. They may be feeling insecure, so tell them they're doing well.

Do say: 'As part of our restructuring, a number of positions will unfortunately be lost. Those no longer needed will be offered the maximum support.'

Don't say: 'UR P45 IS W8NG. LOL.'

DO IT RIGHT: LETTING SOMEONE GO

Know where you stand. Understand fully the rules and legal obligations of employment law and you will minimise the risk of a tribunal. Even if you would win in the end, you will want to avoid the process.

Tell the right people, in the right order. The news absolutely has to come from you. Beware the reach of the rumour mill.

Do it properly. Firing people is unpleasant, but it's part of what you're paid for. Don't do what some employers have done and lay off staff by text message. Offer consultation and take people through the process.

Say it straight. Being vague is as bad as being brutal. Make sure your message is understood. Don't try to stay friends: promising to take them back when things pick up is asking for trouble. Still . . .

Don't make enemies. You never know when your paths will cross again. Turn up for an interview in ten years and the employee you so insensitively let go may be on the panel.

Manage the fallout. A close team will be upset by the loss of a member. Explain why the sacking was necessary, and this should ensure the commitment and enthusiasm of your team in the future.

And what if it happens to you?

Ten Ways to Ride Redundancy

1 Be prepared for it
2 Know your rights
3 Negotiate the best deal
4 Remember: it's no slur on your ability
5 Allow yourself to be upset
6 Take some time out to regroup
7 Work out how it can be a good thing
8 Put yourself about
9 Maintain an upbeat demeanour
10 Do what you've always wanted to do

When redundancies happen, the focus tends to remain on the people leaving, but the aftermath requires delicate and dedicated management to prevent morale sinking to rock bottom. It's the survivors who matter now.

YOUR ROUTE TO THE TOP... NURTURING SURVIVORS

Say it straight. For the survivors of a restructure, one question matters: what happens next? When sharing details of the new way, be candid ('sadly, things can't be as they were') and clear ('the new structure looks like this'). Be prepared to answer all questions.

Get real. If you feel saddened by the restructure, share your distress. Openness and humanity are not signs of weakness.

Show the way. GE's former CEO Jack Welch once said: 'Good business leaders create a vision, articulate the vision [and] passionately own the vision.' Facts will calm fears, but igniting hope and enthusiasm takes much more. Paint a vivid picture of the new world and the exciting opportunities to come.

Get your hands dirty. Your role as leader has just begun. In the inevitable adjustment period of blurred remits and increased workloads, be there to solve problems and plug any gaps. Make your team's transition as smooth as possible.

Pass the power. Move your survivors from angst to action by asking how they can make the change work for themselves. They are more likely to thrive if they're optimistic and take responsibility for meeting challenges.

Set goals. In the midst of a restructuring, it is easy to let the simplest (but most effective) things slide. Setting clear objectives with your survivors will provide focus and direction, while emphasising the need for sustained performance.

Be patient. People quickly adapt to new team structures and processes, but the effects of losing friends can last longer. Curb your eagerness for business as usual and give your people time to heal.

GETTING AHEAD

HAVE A DREAM

Although you're raring to go, becoming a success in your chosen field isn't easy. More than anything else, it's about having the right attitude (being resilient, flexible and determined); and having the patience to build up a successful career over time. How much time do you spend fretting about your next career move? Do you feel stuck in your job? Are you unsure about where to go next? Or worried that you've made a mistake? Relax. No decision is entirely irreversible; and failure can lead you down a more interesting path.

Although you might feel like it's a race, it's not. In fact, it's better to take time to carefully consider each career move than to blindly jump at every opportunity that comes your way, only to regret the decision later. Think marathon rather than sprint. You need to have an ambitious strategy but also the flexibility to take advantage of an opportunity when it arises. The trick is to have the courage of your own convictions.

AIM HIGH

'Ambition is a dream with a V8 engine'
ELVIS PRESLEY SAID IT

When it comes to your career, the higher you aim, the further you will get. There's no point scrabbling around at the lower end of the ambition scale – you have to dare to think big. What have you got to lose? Would you like to become a chief executive of a FTSE plc? Do you want to run your own business? Or manage the New York office? Like Elvis said, you've got to start with a dream – without one, you've got nothing to aim for … just don't gorge yourself on deep-fried hamburgers when you do eventually make it to the top.

WORDS-WORTH: CAREER

Do you worry about your 'career'? Of course you do. Whether you're just starting out, moving along nicely, contemplating a change or planning to wind down, there's always something to fret about. Ideally, a career ought to be steady, controlled and planned. Which is odd, because that's the opposite of what the word originally meant. There's a clue in the matching verb. When a youth in a pimped-up car goes 'careering' down the high street, it's not a steady progression. It's a mad dash. The French carrière, *from which the word derives, meant a racecourse. The ultimate source is the Latin* carrus, *a wagon. In English, from the sixteenth century, it meant a short gallop at high speed, or a cavalry charge. It acquired its present meaning of a professional life in the nineteenth century. Since then, there have been various improvements. In the mid-twentieth century the Americans introduced the idea of 'career men' and 'career girls'. But some will be more interested in a more recent idea: the 'career break'.*

YOUR ROUTE TO THE TOP...
REALISE YOUR DREAM

Immerse yourself in the outcome. Dreams come at a price. So ponder the implications on your other aspirations and the consequence of following your dreams.

Work out the journey. Think clearly through the steps you must take in order to achieve your dream, as well as the dream itself. As Napoleon said: 'Plans are useless, but the act of planning is invaluable.'

Surround yourself with critical friends. Build a network of people who are on your side but will also tell you the truth. Business leaders, past clients and successful entrepreneurs can all act as mentors and guides along the way.

Persist. Keep at it and stick to your guns. Remember: dreams worth realising don't come easy.

Be flexible. Have a broad view of what you wish to achieve, but be prepared to compromise on how you make it happen. Many great inventions, including Coca-Cola and Post-It notes, came as a result of going off-track. By being flexible we often come up with something bigger and better – and sooner.

Timing is everything. Watch for trends, stay close to your audience, be patient and choose your moment carefully. The key to success is to be just ahead of the market but not aeons ahead.

Be happy to fail. There will always be stumbling blocks when undertaking any worthwhile enterprise. Capture the insights, adapt and move on.

Approach it in stages. If it all seems too much and you find yourself stuck, focus on one thing at a time. Break it down into mini-milestones and just work on achieving the next step.

Avoid relying on your dream for self-esteem. When we draw our strength from many different parts of our life we're more likely to have the stamina to keep going.

'Life is too short to be living somebody else's dream'
HUGH HEFNER SAID IT

Hugh Hefner's *Playboy* dream might not be everyone's idea of success but his sentiment is true. You may be lucky enough to know exactly what it is you want to do with your life but it still takes courage to pursue it. And just because you don't know anyone who has made it as a TV producer, a teacher or an investment banker, it doesn't mean *you* can't do it.

Allow yourself the freedom to try something different, to change tack when it's clear you're not happy with the path that you have taken, and to set aside unrealistic expectations. Dreams remain nebulous without concrete goals to anchor them down. However, be warned – goals are useful things but shouldn't be pursued to the detriment of everything else. They must be regularly reviewed and kept realistic. It's easy to lose heart if you're too hard on yourself.

YOUR ROUTE TO THE TOP...
FULFIL YOUR GOALS

Start with overall goals. These may need help from others and depend on things you have no control over; e.g., the Queen's goals might include improving the royal family's reputation.

The best goals are expressed positively. More support for the monarchy rather than less support for a republic.

Support your goals with objectives. Develop a series of aims that concentrate on things that are largely up to you to do.

Look for measures of success. The percentage of the UK population who believe the monarchy is good value for money is a hard measure, but unprompted positive remarks from a range of opinion-formers could be just as useful.

Agree on targets that stretch but don't strain. Define missed goals, successes, mighty successes and 'you must be joking'. Achieving a better reputation than last year is realistic; than any other European head of state is a stretch; than Nelson Mandela may be a step too far.

Discussion is essential. Goals that are imposed or agreed in isolation disappear without trace. Those that are discussed and agreed are more likely to motivate and less likely to be changed.

Imagine what a great month or year would be like. Worry about how to achieve it later.

Publish goals. Others will be more likely to help you achieve them and it will be easier to see where various individuals' efforts overlap or contradict.

Revisit your goals regularly. It's easy to forget what some of them are; a regular check will help you keep on track.

Circumstances change. If goals are to be useful, they'll need to change too. Do this collaboratively. 'I don't mind if the goalposts are moved so long as I'm the one who moved them.'

STAND OUT FROM THE CROWD

If you want your career to take off, you've not only got to aim high but you've also got to get noticed. There's no use doing a brilliant job if no one knows about it. We live in highly competitive times, so having the edge over someone else often boils down to not only being good at what you do, but making sure that those above you know it too. You don't know what opportunities might head your way if you've proved that you can do a good job and have made it clear that you're keen to take on new projects. Remember to say yes to things, even if you're not sure you can do them.

Getting noticed is a subtle art. You can try shouting about your successes to all and sundry, but boasting won't win you any friends — it'll just serve to get up your colleagues' noses. No, getting noticed is a much more sophisticated game. It's as much about being consistently great in the work you do as having the ear of the people who matter. It's also about thinking differently from everyone else: don't be part of the crowd.

YOUR ROUTE TO THE TOP...
HOW TO GET NOTICED

Take the lead. Set the mood rather than follow it. Be more energetic but more measured. Whatever you think is needed to establish the right tone, take charge and you'll be noticed for it.

Challenge conventions. Established systems are there for good reasons, but sometimes rules need to be broken.

Do more than is asked. Volunteer to manage tasks and be responsible for projects. This will win over grateful allies and show colleagues that you're ready to take more on.

Adopt a cause. That might be taking a stance on the office recycling policy or getting involved in local politics. Pick your battles wisely, but make sure you have them from time to time.

Notice the little things. If you see your client's BlackBerry is running low on juice, offer a charger. Or while you wait for colleagues to arrive, recall the conversation you had last time you met. Show you're on the ball with regular little gestures.

Have presence. Don't let people talk over you. If a conversation starts beside your desk, stop and look at them calmly; this shows that you don't want to interrupt them, or by implication, be interrupted yourself. They'll stop and apologise and you can continue where you left off.

Keep on moving if it's the right opportunity. Don't change jobs or roles every couple of years just for the sake of it. But if it's right for you, new challenges will keep you on your toes and employers will have to pay attention if they want to keep up.

Get the right balance. Be humble with your successes and generous with credit: 'This was something I learnt from managing Project Delta in the tricky period before the new clients started to flood in; the work that Mr X did was invaluable to the project.'

Follow up. Do whatever you commit yourself to. Send a follow-up e-mail; invite your client to a suitable event. Once you've got their attention, keep it.

Try to get noticed in everything you do. By concentrating on maximising your impact in your day-to-day dealings with people, you'll gradually build up an excellent reputation.

Ten Ways to Maximise Your Impact

1   Know your goals
2   Trust your strengths
3   Claim credit where it's due
4   Befriend the people with power...
5   ... Know what they like
6   Be confident – say 'yes' to a risk
7   Market yourself shrewdly
8   Volunteer for new projects
9   Dare to be different...
10 ... but be realistic

Combine a great reputation with charm, and you're destined to become a high-flyer...

YOUR ROUTE TO THE TOP...
CHARM YOUR WAY UP

Inspire people. Think Martin Luther King. Appeal to people's emotions by showing them how it could be if only they dared to dream. Your optimism will pull people in.

Share your passion. If you can't find enthusiasm, find an angle. Link the new performance-management system into how you helped your son transform his grades, or how your football team shot up the league. Showing you care brings a topic to life.

Surprise 'em. Russian leader Nikita Khrushchev banged his shoe on the table in response to a speech criticising the Soviet Union's role in Eastern Europe. Unconventional responses to familiar situations get our attention.

Create empathy. Give natural synergy a nudge by consciously matching others. Try speaking at the same volume or pace, and reflect movement. Be subtle though. You'll know it's working when you laugh and they laugh too.

Add some sparkle. Use words that express emotion (excited, nervous, thrilled), evoke sounds (crash, whoop, boom) and be descriptive (immense, shimmering, fierce). Be a wordsmith: use language to change how people feel, not just what they think.

Captivate your audience. Draw people in with positive comparisons: 'Just like you, Ben's always coming up with solutions.' A little flattery goes a long way.

Be generous. Give answers that go beyond what's needed: 'An excellent book – practical as well as an easy read', rather than 'It was fine'. Interesting people share colours and flavours.

THE MANAGEMENT MASTERCLASS

Tell stories. In his victory speech, president-elect Barack Obama told how 'change has come to America' through the eyes of 106-year-old Ann Nixon Cooper. He took the audience on her journey. We felt the 'heartache and the hope; the struggle and the progress' that she did. Next time you hear a good story, note it down. It could come in useful.

GET YOUR DREAM JOB

'Luck is preparation meeting opportunity'
OPRAH WINFREY SAID IT

Standing out from the crowd will never be as important as when you're applying for your dream job. You have to make sure that your CV will knock them out and give a genuine sense of 'you'. But it's the job interview that is the real make-or-break time. It's about preparation, preparation, preparation.

DO IT RIGHT: JAZZ UP YOUR CV

Be concise. A stand-out CV doesn't mean a novella about how great you are.

Stick to the point. Keep it brief and fuss-free; aim for just two pages. No one cares about your life story, apart from your parents.

Don't rely on bullet-points. You may want to list your attributes like an airport departures board, but this can appear stark and robotic – and it's torture to read. Give an idea as to who you are, not just what you've done.

Identify your key skills. If you can rival Stephen Hawking in the maths department or sell fridges to the Inuit, make sure you drive this home.

Avoid gimmicks. A journalism graduate once presented his CV like the front page of a newspaper. He didn't get the job. Using neon paper or attaching your document to a bunch of musical helium balloons will get you noticed, but not for the right reasons.

Get a friend to proofread. Ask your most literate chum to check through your CV. An independent eye can spot mistakes that you may not.

Write a good cover letter. This gives you more opportunity to sell yourself. Avoid standard website letters. Take time and care to write a memorable one-pager, using a formal yet friendly tone and explaining how your skills and experience are relevant to the position.

Don't lie. Gild the lily, yes, but outright untruths could cost you the job if you're caught out at the interview stage or later.

So, you're lucky enough and determined enough to have been given an interview for your dream job. Better not mess it up...

Interview Time: Five killer questions to prepare for

1. 'Tell me about yourself'

There's no set answer to this one, but it's a fair bet that the interviewer does not want to know about your cycling

Ten Ways to Shine at Interview

1 Do your research
2 Dress smartly
3 Be ready for difficult questions
4 Don't ramble, or fear the silence
5 Talk up your skills...
6 ... but be ready to admit weaknesses
7 Smile – but not all the time
8 Ask questions
9 Be yourself...
10 ... but be what they're looking for too

proficiency test aged seven. This is an opportunity to paint a picture that positions you as the ideal candidate; mention anything that you would like to be asked more about.

2. 'Why do you want to work here?'

This question is an invitation to demonstrate that you've thought about different employers, and you've done your research on this organisation. If you can relate it to your own experience, all the better ('I've always used your products and I think they're fabulous'); and explain how this move fits into your career.

3. 'Why did you decide to leave your previous job?'

However tempting, don't launch into a slag-fest against your erstwhile employer. If you say you left this or that job because your employers didn't live up to your expectations, it will make your interviewee think you can't be satisfied and there's nothing they can do to make you a good employee.

4. 'What is your greatest weakness?'

On no account are you to answer 'chocolate biscuits'. Unless the interviewer has a DVD set of *The Office* stashed in his top drawer, he's unlikely to appreciate the joke. Nor, if you are applying for an accountancy role, should your reply be 'working with numbers'. Boringly, identify something relatively innocuous and stress the steps you have taken to remedy this shortcoming.

5. 'How do you respond to criticism?'

This is one question that has a simple answer. 'I use criticism as feedback.' Talk about how you listen to criticism and learn from it, and you'll be ticking the right boxes. Tell the interviewer that you give as good as you get and they'll be rapidly downgrading your prospects.

Maybe you love your organisation but are itching to get ahead. You've grown out of your current role and you want to prove to your boss that you've got what it takes to get to the next level.

YOUR ROUTE TO THE TOP...
HOW TO GET PROMOTED

Go the extra mile. By doing more than is asked for, you'll win grateful colleagues and show that you are ready to take on more.

Network like crazy. The more people you know within your organisation and outside it, the greater your chances of being offered a new role.

Do the detail – but don't talk about it. You want to be seen to be thinking about big issues, not small ones.

Have an opinion. You want to be seen to stand for something. Pick your battles wisely, but make sure that you do have them from time to time.

Enthusiasm is infectious. Show your excitement and commitment to the organisational cause. Those at the top will want you in a role where your energy is influencing others.

Facilitate in meetings. This will set you apart from the rest and makes it less likely that you will end up in a relationship-damaging conflict. You may even be praised as the one who gets the most out of people.

Avoid the well-trodden career route. Tomorrow's leaders will almost certainly have a different set of experiences from today's, and the unorthodox career path will make it harder to compare you with your peers.

Be focused but flexible. Decide on the role you want, the skills you need to do it, and how you can demonstrate you have them. Be open to new chances as they occur.

Have stamina. Staying power is one of the most important yet least recognised attributes of successful leaders. To get to the top, keep going and don't be put off by setbacks. It's a long journey.

ARE YOU SUFFERING FROM... TRANSITION ANXIETY?

We're all supposed to want a promotion more than dear life, but promotion in today's world is considered as stressful as divorce, and about as welcome. Transition Anxiety is the fear of being elevated to a position of responsibility and authority when you were quite happy being irresponsible and

unimportant. It is the sense of knowing that everyone else thinks you don't deserve the promotion and will, from now on, spend their time undermining you. Symptoms include not being able to get out of bed in the morning and avoiding the CEO's call, even though the secretary congratulated you when she put him through. Treatment involves being purposely incompetent until they discover you really are useless, or taking the job and waiting until they de-elevate you back to your old position. Of course, saying 'no, thank you' will rid you of the problem – and the job – once and for all.

THE MANAGEMENT MASTERCLASS

HOT TIPS

'When your dreams turn to dust, vacuum'
DESMOND TUTU SAID IT

Don't fall into the trap of thinking that just because you know where you want to be in five years' time and that you're good at what you do, that the world owes you a living. You're wrong. Sometimes luck collides with ambition and a dream opportunity will fall into your lap – but these golden moments will be few and far between. So, you must cultivate a tough mental attitude that will help you do your best despite all the problems, obstacles and confusions that will muddy your career path. Don't fall at the first hurdle.

Ten Ways to Toughen Up

1. Don't take it personally
2. Believe in yourself
3. Accept it's OK to make mistakes...
4. ... but don't make too many
5. Keep your focus
6. Hold your nerve
7. Don't compare yourself to others
8. Let go of anger
9. Take a few risks
10. Learn to switch off

TEN VITAL TOUGH VALUES

1 Self-belief

Mental toughness is above all else about self-belief. The face that looks back at you from the mirror: do you believe in it? Does it convince you? If you do not possess deep self-belief, you are unlikely to convince anyone else that you're worth listening to or worth following.

2 Resilience

We all have setbacks but you have to come back, and stronger. It is not events in themselves that matter, it is how you react to them and cope with them. You can take risks, experience successes and reverses, but you must always press on to the next challenge. Do not allow the latest quirk of fate or bad luck to shake you from your purpose. There are even shades here – dangerous thought – of Nietzsche's belief: 'That which does not kill me makes me stronger.' Think about that the next time your senior manager is giving you a bollocking.

3 Focus

If you want to be the best, you have got to be totally focused on what you are doing. When you arrive back home at the end of the day and your toddler has a headache and your teenage son has rung up asking for a top-up on his monthly allowance, do you have time to feel sorry for yourself? Or do you get on with preparing for tomorrow's meeting?

4 Drive

This means having an insatiable desire and internalised

motives to succeed. It is a quality that elite sports stars recognise. The motives have to be there for you, and you have to really want it because it's very hard work. Internalised motives provide you with a frame of reference and meaning when the going gets tough.

5   **Control**

You must know how to regain psychological control following unexpected, uncontrollable events. When President George W. Bush went for his morning run on 11 September 2001 he was still just the untested ex-president's son. A few hours later, he was a world leader at one of the most dangerous moments in his nation's history. At a meeting of the key players a few weeks after the al-Qaeda attack, Bush calmed his colleagues' nerves. 'You know what? We need to be patient,' Bush said. 'We've got a good plan. Look, we're entering a difficult phase. The press will seek to find divisions among us. They will try and force on us a strategy that is not consistent with victory. We've been at this only nineteen days. Be steady. Don't let the press panic us. Resist the second-guessing. Be confident but patient … It's all going to work.'

6   **Resolve**

This means pushing back the boundaries of physical and emotional pain, while still maintaining discipline and effort under distress. Generations of rugby coaches have urged their schoolboy charges to 'get in there where it hurts'. In business as well as sport, sometimes you have to take personal risks with your own safety and go through the pain barrier if you are going to achieve anything big. Overcoming the pain of fear or nervousness is the key to success for risk-taking leaders. Only the truly mentally tough can do it.

7 Nerves of steel

It's about accepting that anxiety/pressure is inevitable and knowing that you can cope with it. Accept that you're going to get nervous, particularly when the pressure's on. But keeping the lid on it and being in control is crucial. Mentally tough managers are not fazed by nerves or fear. They can handle the pressure. In fact, they expect it – it goes with the territory of being at the top. It is merely another obstacle to be overcome on the way to success.

8 Independence

You must not be adversely affected by others' good or bad performance. Comparing yourself to others is usually unwise. You will be filled with a sense of either inferiority or superiority. You just have to focus on you and your performance – don't look at others and say: 'I'm not that brave.' The lesson is, concentrate on your own results. Don't measure yourself in terms of other people's achievements.

9 Competitiveness

Mentally tough managers thrive in the pressure of competition – they are able to raise their game when the occasion demands it, no matter what has happened. Mental toughness is being resilient to and using the competition pressure to get the best out of yourself. If the manager has the stomach for a fight, the team will follow.

10 Chillability

This is about switching the focus on and off as required. Knowing when to relax, perhaps in preparation for the next big fight, is another key aspect of mental toughness. The mentally tough performer succeeds by having control of the on/off switch – realising that there are other important things in my life, which deserve my attention … it's important I discipline myself to give them the time. You must be able to leave work behind – take your holidays, enjoy your weekends. Those periods help restore you and make sure you're ready for future challenges.

Having a tough mental attitude is a requirement if you're determined to make your dreams happen. But you also have to realise that no matter how brilliant you are, you can't force things along to suit your own timetable. Patience is a much under-rated virtue but it's the key to long-term success.

YOUR ROUTE TO THE TOP...
SLOW DOWN TO ACHIEVE

Give it all you've got. Direct all your attention to what you're doing now, and do it brilliantly. Don't let your mind rush on to the next task until you've finished this one.

Listen a bit longer. We tend to jump in with an answer before we've got all the information. Letting the other person speak will ensure that they feel heard, and may make them feel more positive about your proposal.

Let other people make the mistakes. The first to market doesn't always succeed. The second and third to market can learn from the lessons of the pioneer and avoid their mistakes for a fraction of the cost.

Learn your habits. Work out where your rushing causes you to make mistakes – leaving your keys at home, your mobile in the office, or your head in the last meeting. Use a prompt as a reminder to slow down. If the shower curtain features in your early-morning rush, use it as a trigger to alert you to take a breath and cut your speed.

Get out of the speed trap. Faster isn't necessarily quicker. Go at a pace that works for you – just because everyone else is rushing doesn't mean that you have to.

Fill dead time. Have something to do while you're standing in a queue or waiting for someone to arrive. Rather than getting impatient, much better to read something you've been meaning to get round to or draft a few letters.

Defer judgement. Get comfortable with not knowing the answer straight away. Be confident enough to say 'I don't know' occasionally, then allow yourself time to find an answer that's right, rather than merely the quickest.

Let your conscious mind work. Take time to mull an idea over. The most innovative thoughts invariably arrive after a period of incubation.

Sometimes you'll find yourself in a real rut. What then? A more radical approach may be needed...

Ten Ways to Reinvent Yourself

1 Take responsibility for where you are now
2 Think: what do I want to be?
3 Work out what's stopping you
4 Enjoy the process
5 Buy some new threads
6 Do something you always said you wouldn't
7 Chat to people you normally ignore
8 Learn to trust your judgement
9 Take life less seriously...
10 ... but put more into it

YOUR ROUTE TO THE TOP...
MAKE A FRESH START

Find your focus. A complete life overhaul may sound exhilarating, but it is usually unnecessary and unrealistic. Recognise your priorities by imagining yourself a year from now – happy and fulfilled. What are you doing? How do you spend your time? How is it different from today? Identify changes that pave a path to the new way, and concentrate solely on them.

Speed through the cycle. Making a change involves moving through four stages (doing, contemplating, planning and experimenting). Locate yourself in the cycle and take action to move yourself forward. Those too busy 'doing' to consider a change, take a day off to think; aimless contemplators, write a plan.

Break it down. Avoid overwhelming paralysis by turning your long-term vision ('I will make a success of this business') into manageable, short-term goals ('I will call ten of my lapsed clients by the end of today').

Up the pressure. Share your plan with colleagues, friends and family members and ask them to keep tabs on your progress. Skipping a week of your new training course won't be so tempting once your pride is at stake.

Remember why. Whether it's the drivers you're now satisfying (independence, challenge), the strengths you're building (leadership, courage), or the passions you're exploring (politics, the arts), there are reasons you made a change. When the going gets tough, don't forget them.

Learn from the greats. Identify people who have achieved what you want to and map your own path to theirs. Worried it's too late to change? Emulate Colonel Harland Sanders, who made his new start (and fortune) at 65. When a motorway development forced him to close his service station, Sanders shunned retirement to secure investment in his fried chicken recipe – and KFC was born. There's still time.

Think back. One you've settled into the new way, reflect on lessons learned. Write down how you overcame challenges, what skills you developed and how you would approach things differently next time. Use it to make future fresh starts swift and stress-free.

WATCH OUT FOR...

Like broken pavement slabs, there are things that will serve to trip you up in your mission to succeed. First up is the tricky world of office politics…

YOUR ROUTE TO THE TOP...
PURE POLITICKING

Play the game. You will find politics in the personality of every organisation. Master the basics and you can win without sacrificing your integrity.

Look, listen and learn. Every company has its own culture, so spend time observing the characteristics. What does success look like here? Which types rise to the top? Are they assertive and creative, or cautious and straight down the line? Emphasise your skills in line with the winners.

Become a cultural chameleon. Don't try to change things, adapt. Whether it's dress, office hours or communication style, be clear on what you can compromise on for long-term gain.

Don't underestimate the power of personality. Your skills are expendable; you are not. Make people appreciate you for your good attitude and cultural fit. Hard work isn't enough.

State your aims. If you want to earn more, speak to your manager about what it will take to secure promotion. Become known for straight talking and people will trust your word.

Make the right contacts. Those who influence decisions and allocate resources are not necessarily the ones at the top. Find out who has fingers in the important pies. Recognition for good work comes naturally when the right people know you.

Develop a power base. E-mailing your boss every time you achieve something says more about your insecurity than your ability. Get to know colleagues at all levels to build support.

Become an expert. Great office politicians are great people-managers. By empathising with colleagues' true motivations, you can negotiate, influence and delegate your way to success.

Manage your reputation. You must be seen to be making a positive impression on everyone, at all times. Control stress levels, downplay poor performance and steer clear of troublemakers. This will win you votes in the long term.

What happens if things do start going your way, and you find yourself being feted as one of the new hot talents? You might be feeling pretty pleased with yourself – but watch out. No one likes working with a self-satisfied bore.

ARE YOU SUFFERNG FROM... TALL POPPY SYNDROME?

The term originates from Livy's *History of Rome*, Book I, which tells the story of Sextus. Sextus put to death all the important people in his town of Gabii after his father Tarquinius Superbus symbolically cut off the heads of all the tall poppies in his garden. The Australians and New Zealanders use this story to support their view that no one should ever get too big for their boots, lest a terrible fate befall them. Although we now live in an era of self-promotion, PR and publicists, one must always seem surprised by and even truly sorry for one's success. Besides, we all know that anyone who believes their own myth has a series of much worse syndromes to contend with. Treatment for Tall Poppy Syndrome is twofold: either resign from the top job and be a loser like everyone else, or get used to the view from above. But whatever you do, never tell anyone how much fun you're having.

Ten Ways to Get Ahead in Business

1   Concentrate on what you do best
2   Be enthusiastic – it's contagious
3   Talk to people with experience
4   Take short-term pain for long-term gain
5   Under-promise and over-deliver
6   When you're ready, take the big risk
7   Avoid time-wasters – they shorten life
8   The harder you fall, the harder you become
9   Take 'no' as a diversion, not a stop sign
10 Never get personal unless it's personal

MORE TO
EXPLORE

BIBLIOGRAPHY

Paul Arden (2006), *Whatever You Think, Think the Opposite*, Penguin

Linda Babcock & Sara Laschever (2008), *Ask For It*, Piatkus Books

Stephen Bayley & Roger Mavity (2007), *Life's a Pitch...*, Bantam Press

Jeremy Bullmore (2006), *Another Bad Day at the Office?*, Penguin

Business Essential (2009), A&C Black

Jim Collins (2001), *Good to Great*, Random House

Stephen R. Covey (2004), *The Seven Habits of Highly Effective People*, new edition, Simon & Schuster

Richard Donkin (2009), *The Future of Work*, Palgrave Macmillan

William Essex (2006), *Can I Quote You on That?*, Harriman House Publishing

Howard Gardner (2006), *Five Minds for the Future*, Harvard Business School Press

Rob Goffee & Gareth Jones (2006), *Why Should Anyone Be Led by You?*, Harvard Business School Press

Malcolm Gladwell (2008), *Outliers*, Allen Lane

Daniel Goleman (1996), *Emotional Intelligence*, Bloomsbury Publishing

Gary Hamel with Bill Breen (2007), *The Future of Management*, Harvard Business School Press

Charles Handy (2007), *Myself and Other More Important Matters*, Arrow

Julia Hobsbawm (2009), *The See-Saw*, Atlantic Books

W.J. King with James Skakoon (2008), *The Unwritten Laws of Business*, Profile Books

Manage Projects Successfully (2009), A&C Black

Managing in a Downturn (2009), FT/Prentice Hall

Corinne Mills (2009), *You're Hired! CV*, Trotman

The Mind Gym (2005), *Wake Up Your Mind*, Sphere

The Mind Gym (2006), *Give Me Time*, Time Warner Books

The Mind Gym (2009), *Relationships*, Sphere

Henry Mintzberg (2009), *Managing*, FT/Prentice Hall

Blaire Palmer (2009), *The Recipe For Success*, A&C Black

Stephen Palmer & Cary Cooper (2007), *How to Deal With Stress,* Kogan Page

Philip Ramsden (2008) *Figures Mundane and Mysterious*, Teach Yourself

Richard Reeves & John Knell (2009), *The 80 Minute MBA*, Headline Business Plus

Carole Stone (2004), *The Ultimate Guide to Successful Networking*, Vermilion

Succeed as a New Manager, revised edition (2009), A&C Black

Leigh Thomson (2007), *The Truth About Negotiations*, Prentice Hall

Avivah Wittenberg-Cox & Alison Maitland (2009), *Why Women Mean Business*, John Wiley & Sons

PICTURE CREDITS

We would like to thank the following for kindly supplying material for use in this book:

Getty Images – pp. 33, 40, 49, 57, 84, 96, 134
iStock – pp. 117, 121, 155, 169
Mirrorpix – p.42
Patrick Regout – pp. 29, 34, 59, 75, 78, 81, 92, 101, 110, 125, 139, 151, 164

INDEX

Note: Page numbers in bold denote major sections.